# Coffin Corner

*The True Story of Kenneth Horrigan,*
*World War II POW in Stalag 17B*

Kenneth V. Horrigan

**Eloquent Books**

Eloquent Books
An imprint of Strategic Book Group
P.O. Box 333
Durham CT 06422
www.StrategicBookGroup.com

ISBN: 978-1-60911-011-6

Printed in the United States of America

# The "Coffin Corner..."

We, the smaller and lighter two-engine, B-26 Bombers had much more maneuverability than the bigger, heavier bombers and if necessary we could get in a very, very tight formation, almost wing tip to wing tip. It was in a step pattern from front to back, so that the lead plane's bombs wouldn't fall on the following planes. And that step pattern followed progressively from front of the formation to the rear.

Unfortunately, the antiaircraft fire (ack-ack) was always a problem. You just couldn't believe how those Germans got so good. We are at ten or fifteen thousand feet, flying at 150 to 200 mph. And in about thirty seconds, they could put that stuff right up in our formation. Thank God it took those thirty seconds for the shell to get up there, because then we had the time to employ evasive action. We knew that those shells would be blasting us if we kept flying in a straight line, so we turned about forty-five degrees (maybe right initially, then forty-five degrees to the left). If we looked out to see where we would have been if we had kept in a straight line, there were the ack-ack bursts, right there! But the whole formation never got completely out of the way; the planes on the far outside of the formation sometimes remained in harm's way. Those outside planes in the formation were called the "coffin corner." Each time we had a flight, we were assigned a different spot in the formation. Our crew members knew that, eventually, we would be assigned the "coffin corner."

Our crew lucked out for ten missions. Then on our eleventh mission, we got assigned the "coffin corner." Particularly for us, that was the appropriate name for that position in the formation. Normally the ack-ack, when it explodes, makes a woofing sound. But all of a sudden, on this mission, one of the woofing sounds turned into a BANG.! A shell went through our right engine. I looked around, and there were glass shards everywhere. Also, the right bay window was broken.

Then Bill, the top turret gunner, calls down to me and says, "Get me down." I pull the cord to let him down and ask if he is all right. He says he's got shrapnel in his left leg. I said I didn't think it was so bad, but he says look up in the turret. I look up and it is practically blown away. Our interphone network wasn't working, so the bombardier/navigator (he did both) comes back and says, "Put your parachutes on—we have to bail out." He had come through the bomb bay on a little catwalk while the doors were open and after the bombs had been jettisoned. Pretty scary.

# Dedication

*This book is dedicated to my mom, Betty Horrigan, Kenneth's wife of forty years, and mother to my sisters, Colleen, Mary, Shaune, and Anne. She has not been with us for the last twenty-five years, losing her long battle with Parkinson's disease when she was only sixty-two.*

*Mom was by far Kenneth's primary supporter throughout the forty years they were together. In fact, she may have been the primary reason Dad was able to live and function almost normally even after suffering the emotional trauma he experienced during the war. Dad hid inside himself emotions he never wanted to expose, and mom made it easy for him. Together they came to enjoy the simple things in life and she never expected more of him than he could give. When his jobs came and went, and "this guy" or "that guy" was "out to get him," Mom was unfazed. She took him for his word and never really worried about his outside successes. She was just always glad to see him when he came home.*

*As a small child, the highlight of our day was when Dad was coming home. Every day as the afternoon turned into evening Mom would get excited about Dad "coming home soon!" When he got home it was always an exciting time with romping and laughter until dinnertime came. To my mom, Ken was a hero. And to us, his small children, he was our hero too.*

*Cherie Horrigan-Happy, Daughter to Kenneth*

# Contents

# Introduction

—*Cherie Horrigan-Happy*,
Daughter to Kenneth

When my dad came home from the war, he refused to talk about what happened to him in the German prison camp. I heard this from my grandma, my mother, and my aunts and uncles. I remember asking my dad about it over the years, and he would just say nothing.

Then, around 1999, my daughter got a school project to write about anyone in her family who had been in World War II. So she called my dad, who was living in Florida at the time. The next thing we knew, she received about five handwritten pages by fax!

A few years later, at a family party in Michigan, a retired journalist was talking to my dad, and he began making an audio recording of dad's stories of the war. This journalist was very earnest in telling us to record my dad's story.

And recently, at a gathering of friends who work in the advertising business, my dad started talking about his war experiences, and before long he had a large group surrounding him, fascinated by his stories. He is a very entertaining story-teller, with lots of excitement in his voice, along with sound effects. Now that I think of it, this storytelling thing must run in the family. Whenever my grandpa or my dad started talking, people gathered around them!

Not only were there middle-aged people in this advertising crowd, but also young people, people in their early twenties who had never personally known any-one who had been in World War II. It was the young people who were especially interested in his stories and who kept asking him to tell more and more! In this group were several advertising executives and television producers from Chicago who urged me to document my dad's war experiences.

So, I asked my dad to write down what he could remember. I also asked his sister to write about her relationship with him. Put together, this is the story of Kenneth Horrigan, World War II prisoner of war in Stalag 17B.

# A Sister Admires Her Military Brothers

Today I am starting to write some remembrances of my experiences as a little girl living in an American household where my four older brothers left home to fight in World War II. My oldest brother, Tim Horrigan, was a medical doctor and served in the army. My second brother was Bob Horrigan, a graduate of the Annapolis Naval Academy. My third brother was Jack Horrigan, who was a pilot in the Army Air Force. And Ken Horrigan, my youngest brother, also was in the American Air Force. They were all about ten years older than I and seemed to be accomplished, capable, wonderful guys. This chapter is about how I was affected by their leaving home and joining the military service.

My oldest brother Tim graduated from Wayne State University in Detroit, Michigan. He interned at Providence Hospital and became an anesthesiologist. He worked after his graduation from Medical School as an Army Medical Doctor for two years during the war, attending to wounded soldiers returning from the war. He died at age thirty-six from an aneurysm in the brain.

My brother Bob was appointed to attend Annapolis in 1939, but because of the war, his class graduated one year early in 1942. Bob was on the battleship Arkansas, where he made seven trips across the Atlantic. He also served on the battleship California while in the Pacific area of conflict (Historical Documents & Images, pp. D1–2).

1

Jack joined the Army Air Force and trained in Oklahoma. After he got his wings, he stayed in Oklahoma and became an instructor, teaching other fighter pilots. He was stationed there until the end of the war (Historical Documents & Images, pp. D3–5).

Kenneth enlisted in the Air Force at a young age and was stationed in Saginaw, Michigan. I still have a vivid memory of an airplane crash at the base where Ken was stationed. It was headlined in the Detroit newspaper, and I remember my dad hiding the newspaper from my mom so she wouldn't see it. But she found it anyway and had a panic attack, running all over the house. They told me to go get something at the store. So I rode my bike very fast and was home in about ten minutes. Then the phone rang; it was Ken calling to say that he was all right.

I also remember being outside when the planes flew over our house on their way overseas to England.

But most of all, I remember Sunday, December 7, 1941. I was about eight-years-old. I was at a friend's house when it was broadcast that Pearl Harbor had been bombed. I ran home and realized that something terrible had happened. The next thing I remember was President Franklin Roosevelt announcing that we were at war. That was when he proclaimed, "This day will live in infamy."

The overall atmosphere in our house much of the time was tension. Mom didn't like President Roosevelt, who was running for his third or fourth term as president, because she said her boys would go to war. And she was right. All of her fine sons went to war. But my dad was so proud of his wonderful sons that we had four blue stars in our four front windows (Historical Documents & Images, p. D6).

I vividly remember when we received a telegram that my brother Ken was missing in action (Historical Documents & Images, pp. D7–10). The house became somber and pensive. I found Mom crying a lot. I was in the third grade at St. Brigit's School, where we offered prayers every day for Ken. Then I came home one day and Mom opened a letter. It was from the pilot of Ken's plane (Historical Documents & Images, pp. D11–12). He wrote that he saw two parachutes open as they left the plane. The pilot also was able to parachute out of the plane and was rescued by the French Underground and had gotten back to England. That news gave us hope that Ken may be all right. Later we got word that Ken was a prisoner of war (Historical Documents & Images, p. D13). Mom and I started sending CARE packages to Ken. He was in Stalag 17B prisoner of war camp for two and a half years. Our prayers were answered. He was alive. The tension in our house lessened, and life became somewhat normal (Historical Documents & Images, pp. D14–16).

I remember sitting on the front porch watching my dad reading the paper, following the war in the Pacific, where the Americans were hopping from island to island fighting the Japanese. We were grateful when America dropped the atomic bomb on Japan, because we knew the war would soon be over.

I also vividly remember walking into the kitchen the day Ken came home. He was sitting at our kitchen table. He looked very young to me. He was only about twenty-two years old, but for all he had experienced, he was the same wonderful, humble, nice, friendly, funny brother I always knew. He never seemed bitter about his wartime experience.

I'm so glad Cherie asked Ken to write about his experiences while he was a prisoner of war, because he didn't talk about them much. Now, since reading Ken's remembrance, I really feel I know him better.

All of my wonderful brothers and my father were good, loyal, faithful men. They were all part of what is known as the Greatest Generation. They deserve that title. They will always remain heroes in my heart.

*Dorothy LeBlanc Horrigan*

# A Soldier Finally Tells His Story

Here's my story. I'll start with our flight overseas.

We flew a B-26 Martin Marauder—called the Flying Prostitute (I'll explain later)—to our final destination, our home base, near Chelmsford, England, just northeast of London, in preparation for raids on the continent. The Germans were expecting an invasion of American forces and so were creating gun installations in France, Belgium and the Netherlands.

Our missions would be to bomb the gun installations and the railroad marshalling yards in those countries. The planes we would be flying, B-26s, couldn't get to Germany from our base because we were a medium-sized plane and didn't have enough fuel capacity to go to a target beyond these countries and then return to our home base in England.

Before I go much further, I will explain why the B-26 was called the Flying Prostitute. In its original design, the plane had a wingspan that was six feet shorter than the ultimately redesigned plane that I flew in. Apparently, its original design included a shorter wingspan for less air resistance and, therefore, more speed. But that turned into a problem, because in takeoffs it very often lost flying speed and wing support and crashed into the sea. The original training field was in Tampa, Florida, The Mac Dill Air Force Base, just next to the Bay. They now say there are a lot of B-26s on the bottom of Tampa Bay off the end of the runway. The planes took off, then lost flying speed and wing support and crashed into the bay. Now if you look closely at the B-26—the original design—you could see that it didn't have enough wingspan. Therefore, it was nicknamed the Flying Prostitute because, like a prostitute, it had no visible means of support.

Much of my training for combat took place in Kalamazoo, Michigan, not far from my family's home in Detroit, Michigan. One of the events that took place on a regular basis during training was that our group would fall out in formation on the airfield to hear a short formal speech, some patriotic songs, etc. Then one or two of our base camp planes from the bomber group would "buzz" us. That is, they would take off and fly at a very low altitude—100 or 200 feet—beyond our site, so that we couldn't see them until they were very near our formation on the airfield. Then they buzzed us, at high speed. The roar of those planes just over our heads rocked the earth. I assumed this was to inspire us; it was spectacular. We knew and anticipated that every time we had a field formation that we were going to be buzzed.

Then, early one morning we had one of those formations. It was kind of chilly that day (maybe even considered cold), but the routine was the same. We anticipated the buzz job, but it never came. It took me a while to realize that maybe one of those planes was in trouble, and at low altitude that's *real* trouble. Suddenly we saw a cloud of dust and smoke in a shallow valley, a few miles away. Of course, the whole crew was lost. I always wondered, *Could the cold weather have been part of the failure of that aircraft; could the engines not have been warmed up long enough prior to take off?*

We all knew that the news of the accident would be in the local Detroit newspapers.

I learned a number of years later that the *Detroit News* (the local newspaper) reported the crash of a military plane at Kellogg Field. I understand that my father had received the paper early in the morning, saw the report of the crash, and hid the paper so my mother wouldn't see it. However, she *did* find it and knew of the crash. Then, I inadvertently did something that made a bad situation worse.

Since Kalamazoo was not far from my family's home in Detroit, when I got a couple of days off, I would take a short train trip back home. I never called home to tell them I was coming; I didn't think it was necessary. For some reason that I don't remember, I was rescheduled and wouldn't be going home the weekend following the crash. Thinking that my family would be worried if I didn't show up, I decided to call to let them know in advance. This turned into a disaster. I was unaware that it was normal military routine that the base telephone operator was required to place all outside calls himself. When he called my home, my mother answered, and he said, "This is Kellogg Air Force Base calling…" I was on the phone and could hear my mother scream! She dropped the phone and I could hear her running around screaming… She, of course, thought they were calling to report that I had been lost in the aforementioned crash. Then my brother Tim picked up the phone and I hollered right over the operator, "Tim! Tim! This is Ken! I'm okay! Tell Mom I'm okay!" Unfortunately, it wasn't soon enough; my mother suffered a terrible trauma on that day.

So now, back to the flight overseas.

Our original training for combat—practicing with the new Norton Bomb Site, Air Gunnery School, and various other aspects of air war—took place in Kalamazoo, Michigan, so that is where we took off for our ultimate destination, England, by a somewhat southern circuitous route. At the last minute, just before we were about to take off, the navigator we'd been working with was replaced with an apparently more experienced navigator, since portions of this trip were getting to be precarious. An inexperienced navigator could get us off the track, and the itinerary for this trip didn't allow for going off track.

It was February of 1944. We took off from Michigan in snowy winter weather, flying to Georgia (I think Atlanta), which was about 560 miles (Historical Documents & Images, pp. D17–19).

We arrived to a beautiful, warm and sunny day down there, after having left the cold and snowy weather in Michigan. Then we were off to Miami, Florida—about 620 miles. Then to Haiti (Port-au-Prince), which was about 730 miles. Then to Trinidad—about 890 miles. But that was just a fuel stop, as I can remember. So we must have stopped on the northern coast of South America, maybe in Suriname or Guiana, because our next stop was Belem, Brazil, which is about 1,260 miles from Trinidad and a little bit too far to go, not having had a fuel consumption test.

Our plane never had the fuel test before this initial flight—the only one in our group in Battle Creek that didn't—because ours was a new plane, and parts were taken for use in other planes' tests. Our plane's flight was unexpectedly moved up, and we didn't have time for the test. So we had to depart without knowing exactly how far the plane could go on a full tank of fuel. (Maybe this is why we were assigned a more experienced navigator.) So, we traveled from Belem, Brazil, to Natal, Brazil, about 960 miles (Historical Documents & Images, pp. D20–23). Natal is on the most easterly part of Brazil and as close as we can get to Ascension Island, which is way out (1,300 or 1,400 miles) in the South Atlantic Ocean.

So here we are at Natal, ready to fly to Ascension Island, approximately 1,400 miles eastward out in the South Atlantic, the only dry land within a thousand miles of this point, not knowing for sure if our plane had the fuel to complete the trip. If our plane burns more fuel than the norm, then we never make it to the island. Or if our navigation is a little bit off (it's a small island), we won't have enough fuel left to go circulating around to find it. So, I was a little bit apprehensive at this time. But there is nothing I can do except ride along and hope and pray we make it. Just our luck, on the day of our departure, the skies are overcast, and there is no way we can keep our eyes peeled to maybe spot a small island in the ocean because we are above the clouds. Eventually, the navigator says the island should be near here. But the only way he could figure that is by sun shots and/or speed and flight direction and wind speed and direction. None of those methods are really that accurate. But we drop below the clouds, and there off the right wing is Ascension Island surrounded by beautiful blue-green ocean waters. And for me, I mean, that was beautiful (Historical Documents & Images, p. D24)!

Next, we head north to England. That's a long way, with a lot of land and ocean and enemy territory along the way. So, we take off going northeasterly to the Ivory Coast of Africa, landing in (I think) Ghana. But that's about 1,350 miles from Ascension Island, so it could have been Cote D'Ivoire or Liberia, both of which are about a couple of hundred miles closer to Ascension. At any rate, we already knew that our plane had a good fuel consumption rating, based on our flight from South America to Ascension, so it still could have been Ghana. We have no serious incidents on this flight until the pilot requests landing instructions, by radio, from the airport.

Lo and behold, we can't get a radio signal from the airfield. There must be something wrong with our radio transmitter. And guess who's got the job of radio operator and mechanic on this flight? Me! So the pilot calls back to me and says, "I can't get the ground station for landing instructions. Fix the radio transmitter, and fast, because we can't keep circling around here for long—we'll run out of fuel!"

We had three radio transmitters in the plane for the various radio frequencies that any particular airfield may be operating on, and prior to our takeoff from Ascension Island, I had changed our plane's radio frequency to match the frequency this particular airport was operating on. So I checked a couple times the frequency that I had set up for, and it was all right. Here we are, circling at ten thousand feet over Africa, and I'm supposed to pull out, open, and repair a radio transmitter while we are in flight! *No way.* But I figure, at least I can try. So I reach back behind the transmitter to disconnect the wire attachments, so I could pull the unit out. When I touch the terminal that would disconnect the antenna wire, I hear a very slight transmission from the ground station. (My hand and body were apparently acting as a weak antenna.) Then, when I got my head around to look behind the transmitter at the connection, I found that whoever had installed this particular unit had inserted the wire connection too far through the terminal, so that just the insulation of the wire was touching the terminal. Prior to this, both the pilot and I had set our volumes to maximum in an effort to pick up anything we could get from the ground station. When I pulled the wire back so that a proper connection was made, the volume almost blasted our ears off! Needless to say, we then got our landing instructions, landed safely, and everything was okay.

Yeah, everything was okay, but this field was very sparse. Then they had us taxi out to a remote part of the airfield, kind of in the boonies. This country, at that time, was primarily native African tribes. They were not particularly friendly with the white man, and I remembered hearing there were cannibalistic tribes in some parts of Africa. So the pilot figures someone should stay with the plane overnight so that no one ransacks it. Guess who he picks to stay with the plane? And then I wonder – is the pilot giving me this detail because of the problem with the radio and the blast that nearly blew his ears off? I do. They give me a cot and blanket to set up just underneath the front wheel. So I'm laying there, all alone, half asleep, just after the sun sets, and then I hear rhythmic drums—BOOM, BOOM—somewhere, further off in the boonies. Of course, the sound is coming from native tribe members, doing their thing. I'm a little scared, thinking, *I hope they are friendly!* I finally got to sleep that night, somehow. The next morning everything is okay. I'm ready to continue our journey further north on our trip to England.

Our next stop is Casablanca, Morocco, but it's a long way. It's almost two thousand miles as the crow flies. So we had to stop overnight and refuel along the west coast of Africa; I think it was Dakar.

When we did finally get to Casablanca, I seem to remember that we stayed a little bit longer than the standard overnight stop. I guess that's because our next flight was a long way (1,300 or 1,400 miles) over land and ocean and close to enemy territory (occupied France at that time). We made a precursory check of the plane prior to takeoff to be sure that everything was okay. We had to fly a couple hundred miles west of France to avoid enemy fighter attack. Our planes were unarmed, so if attacked, we were defenseless and vulnerable. In other words, we would be sitting ducks. Our route would take us west of England (due to having to go a couple hundred miles west of France) and then turn east to a field in West England. The next day, we continued easterly to our future home base near Chelmsford, England.

That day we all had a great meal in the officers' mess hall, I guess because we all had just completed a precarious journey across the ocean. That was the first and last time I ever had a meal in the officers' quarters.

I think this is the proper time to talk about coming into England from the west. Before we left the States, we had a briefing about just that… "coming into England from the west." The air force had good information that one of the bombers on its overseas flight had landed in a German airfield in Belgium.

It was completely intact—a brand new airplane, never having dropped a bomb nor shot a gun. This was the first time that the air force was made aware of the jet stream, that strong wind (150-200 mph) that often exists high in the stratosphere. Apparently a bomber (I think a B-17) was flying into England from the west when England was overcast with a thick cloud cover (as was usual). The plane had taken the northern air route—I think over Canada, Greenland, and Iceland—and ultimately from the west into England. The navigator, figuring the plane was flying at the normal cruising speed of about 150 mph, told the pilot to break down through the clouds when (flying at that speed) the plane would have been close to their intended destination—an air field in England. Of course, the navigator was unaware of the jet stream (as was everyone at the time) and was actually flying at about 300 or 350 mph, which is 150 mph cruising speed of the plane plus the 150-200 mph jet stream speed. At that speed, the plane had overshot England and was actually over Belgium. The pilot called down to the airfield for landing instructions (in English). And he got a reply (in English), directing him to a runway they had just lit up. They landed and got out of the plane to be immediately surrounded by German soldiers. The Germans got a brand new airplane and the aircrew was sent to various German prison camps.

Of course, they were briefing us to be aware of the jet stream so the same thing didn't happen to us. Later, there was a rumor that one of that crew was in our camp (Stalag 17B), and when he was particularly teed off, he would curse "that g – – d navigator."

So now, back to what and why we went through all of the above—to drop some bombs on some enemy targets.

Of course, we had a few training flights in England prior to combat over enemy territory. These were uneventful. Nothing very unusual happened. The training flights in England were very similar to the one's we had done back home, in Kalamazoo, Michigan, because we were flying over England and would not encounter any enemies (Historical Documents & Images, pp. D25–29).

The training flights were soon over and we were in combat over the European continent. Most of the raids were on railroad marshaling yards, and we only needed standard size bombs to knock out the tracks, thus disrupting the transportation of their material and supplies. We also had a number of raids on the gun emplacements on the shoreline of France and Belgium in their anticipation of an invasion. These gun emplacements were heavy concrete bunkers. To knock them out, we had to use big bombs (called blockbusters), and we had to have a direct hit. These blockbusters were huge. I'm guessing they were three or four feet in diameter and five feet or more in length. They were so big that we could get only two of them in the bomb bay, one on each side of the catwalk. When we took off with these big monster blockbuster bombs, I always kind of wondered if we'd ever get off the ground. I used to stand just behind the pilot and copilot seats, and before we'd begin our roll down the runway, they'd push the accelerators of both engines all the way up to the maximum—while holding the plane at a standstill until it was vibrating and shaking—before they released the brakes and let her go. That, of course, was to get as much speed as we could before they attempted to take off. Then when we did take off, they held the plane in level flight to gain as much speed as possible before climbing over the trees at the end of the field and to a higher elevation. Obviously, we always made it, as is evident by the fact that I'm still here. But I was always kind of apprehensive (Historical Documents & Images, pp. D30–31).

In my capacity as a radio operator, I was located forward of the bomb bay, just behind the pilot and copilot. And in my capacity as a gunner, my position was behind the bomb bay, near two fifty-caliber machine gun emplacements, one on each side of the plane. Of course, when we got into combat, my position was to be between those two gun emplacements, in case of attack by enemy fighters—which never happened.

We all had to wear life vests in case we had to ditch in the English Channel, which could happen as a result of plane damage after a raid or engine trouble. The life vests were not inflated; if and when necessary, we had to pull a little rip chord to inflate them. So on this particular raid, with the two blockbusters in the bomb bay (we were going after their gun emplacements on the shore line), and after crossing over the Channel, I have to go back to my two fifty-caliber guns at the rear of the plane through the bomb bay, along the catwalk between the two monster blockbuster bombs. There's not much room. As I'm going through the bomb bay, my rip cord to the life vest gets caught on a support of the catwalk and is pulled, thereby inflating my life vest and hanging me up in the bomb bay. I'm thinking, *If I can't free myself from this hang-up before we get over the target, they're going to drop those bombs and me with them!* I panicked a little bit, but finally got loose. If we had to ditch that day, I'm not sure my damaged vest would have stayed inflated.

So now for the other raid that stands out in my mind. It was the IJmuiden boat works in the Netherlands (funny spelling—two capital first letters). Actually, it was a German submarine repair port where they took care of their submarine fleet, a major part of the German Navy. It was extremely well fortified, with about a ten-foot solid concrete roof to protect the facility. Somehow our air crews were made aware that our next raid was going to be IJmuiden. We also knew that a heavy bomber group had made a low-level raid on IJmuiden and that the Germans put up a wall of artillery in front of them, including ack-ack that the group had to fly through. The rumor was that all of the planes were lost. This was a nice thing to know, just before our flight, right? Of course, we had to use blockbuster bombs to get through that concrete roof. Apparently, the air force bigwigs (the outfit that plans the raids) learned something from that raid, because we were sent in at a much higher elevation—ten thousand feet. As I can remember, we got through that raid okay. A couple of damaged planes were all. So that was the other raid that stands out in my mind, because I was a little apprehensive prior to that raid. I happened to see a documentary on television recently about that facility, and none of the few bombs that did hit the facility got through the roof, even though those bombs were blockbusters.

We, the smaller, lighter, and more maneuverable two-engine, B-26 Bombers (while in formation over enemy territory) never had a problem with enemy fighters, as did the larger, heavier, four-engine B-17 and B-24 bomber groups. I think it was probably for three good reasons.

First, because the heavy and larger bombers had much more fuel capacity than we did and could fly deep into enemy territory; and therefore, were over enemy territory much longer than we were. That, of course gave the enemy fighters much more time to take off, assemble into a group, locate the heavy B-24 and B-17 American bomber groups, and attach their formations. They didn't have enough time to do that with our B-26 bomber groups because we were in there and out, in a relatively much shorter time period than the heavier bomber groups.

Second, the German enemy fighter planes were capable of flying much faster than our heavy B-17 and B-24 bombers, and because of that excessive speed, they were able to fly circles around our bomber formations. If they thought they could get a tactical advantage, they would fly over, under, above, adjacent to, around, and even through the B-17 or the B-24 formations. Also, the enemy fighters, with their excessive speed, made it very difficult for our bomber crews (with their 50-caliber machine guns) to get a good site (or bead) on the enemy fighters.

Third, the heavy bomber maneuverability was very slow, and for that reason they had to leave a relatively wide space between each other for fear of running into their own bombers. I never flew with a heavy bomber group; I got most of this information while I was in a prison camp (Stalag17b) where there were a lot of heavy bomber crewmembers who had been shot down in one raid or another.

Now, in conjunction with the above, I'll try to analyze in more detail why we, the lighter, faster, and more maneuverable bombers, were not attacked by enemy fighters.

First, the speed of our lighter bombers was pretty close to the speed of the enemy fighters, and if they tried to attack us we would have a sufficient amount of time to get a good site and draw a sharp bead on them. Also, because of our tight formation, if an enemy fighter attacked, the crew members of most of our planes in our formation would be able to get a good site on him with our 50-caliber machine guns, and with all those guns from our nine-plane formation on him, the enemy pilot would quickly be in serious trouble.

Second, we had much more maneuverability than the bigger, heavier bombers and if necessary we could get in a very, very tight formation, almost wing tip to wing tip. The enemy fighter could never fly through this nice, tight formation, which looked somewhat as follows:

It was in a step pattern from front to back, so that the lead plane's bombs wouldn't fall on the following planes. And that step pattern followed progressively from the front of the formation to the rear.

However, the antiaircraft fire (ack-ack) was a different story. All of the military targets were fortified with numerous heavy ack-ack fire batteries. If we flew (our formation) in a straight line toward or over a target—let's say for thirty seconds—that ack-ack would be at our elevation and right in the middle of our formation.

You just couldn't believe how they got so good. We are at ten or fifteen thousand feet, flying at 150 to 200 mph. And in about thirty seconds, they could put that stuff right up in our formation. Thank God it took those thirty seconds for the shell to get up there, because then we had the time to employ evasive action. We knew that those shells would be blasting us if we kept flying in a straight line, so we turned about forty-five degrees (maybe right initially, then forty-five degrees) to the left. If we looked out to see where we would have been if we had kept in a straight line, there were the ack-ack bursts, right there! But the whole formation never got completely out of the way; the planes on the far outside of the formation sometimes remained in harm's way. Those outside planes in the formation were called the "coffin corner." Each time we had a flight, we were assigned a different spot in the formation. Our crew members knew that, eventually, we would be assigned the coffin corner (Historical Documents & Images, p. D32).

But right here I should explain that just prior to our flying over the target, we had to fly in a straight line so the bombardier could line up his bomb site; make adjustments for flying speed, altitude, and wind drift; open the bomb bay doors; and so on. He actually took over the flight of the plane to get precise readings. This was called "the bomb run." It was precarious, and for that reason, he had to make it as short as possible—preferably drop the bombs, turn, and get out of there before the ack-ack shells got up there.

Our crew lucked out for ten missions. Then on our eleventh mission, we got assigned the coffin corner. Particularly for us, that was the appropriate name for that position in the formation. Normally the ack-ack, when it explodes, makes a woofing sound. But all of a sudden, on this mission, one of the woofing sounds turned into a *bang*. A shell went through our right engine. I looked around, and there were glass shards all around. Also, the right bay window was broken.

Then Bill, the top turret gunner, calls down to me and says, "Get me down." I pull the cord to let him down and ask if he is all right. He says he's got shrapnel in his left leg. I said I didn't think it was so bad, but he says look up in the turret. I look up and it is practically blown away. Our interphone network wasn't working, so the bombardier/navigator (he did both) comes back and says, "Put your parachutes on—we have to bail out." He had come through the bomb bay on a little catwalk while the doors were open and after the bombs had been jettisoned. Pretty scary.

Then he goes to the open bomb bay and bails out. I watch him dropping down in a delayed jump (as we were instructed to do). This is so because it's harder for the enemy troops on the ground to see us bailing out, and after that delay, maybe we can land without having been seen by the enemy soldiers—and get in the French underground. Anyway, I watch Lou going down in his delayed jump and I think to myself, *I'm not going to do that! It's too scary!* Then the tail gunner jumps, and then Bill, the top turret gunner, gets in the window to jump, but he hesitates. So I say, "Go, Bill, go!" But he continues to hesitate. And then the plane kind of jerks, as though the pilot was having a tough time controlling it with one engine. You don't want to be in a plane when it's out of control. The excessive centrifugal forces are extreme, and you can't get out. So I give Bill a little nudge and he's out. Now it's my turn, and out I go. I don't want to pull a delayed jump like Lou did, so I pull the rip cord almost as soon as I'm out. But I'm going as fast as the plane was going (more than 100 mph), and the chute opens out on a horizontal plane behind me. Then

I swing down and around (like a pendulum), with the chute in front of me now, and the plane's slipstream collapses the chute. I kind of think to myself, *Wow, I did that wrong.* Then as I swing back down underneath the chute, it opens up again. *Wow, that was close.*

I'm floating down in my parachute, and I look back and see the plane that I had been through so much with flying away on one engine—and I'm floating down here over France. Suddenly, while I'm in the air, I think, *Wow, this is April 22! My brother Jack is getting married today. He's having a ball, and I'm floating down under a parachute somewhere here in France.* I then look down and see that I'm going to land in a wooded area. Uh-oh, I don't want to get hung up in a tree and all the problems that could cause. Looking down, I see a clearing just adjacent to the wooded area. So, I, a hotshot parachute expert, figure I know how to slip a chute. I pull a couple of chords and see that it's working. Then I pull harder and slip into the clearing.

Relaxing, I hit ground, the way I was instructed so that I don't break my legs. I land in the clearing, but right in the middle of a dirt road. Then I'm thinking that they had told me I probably would have a couple minutes before anyone who may have seen me coming down would find me. I was to bundle up my chute and hide it in some weeds and brush, so whoever saw me coming down would not immediately know where I had landed. So, I'm not in any immediate rush, and I start leisurely picking up my chute. Then I hear from the adjacent wooded area, "Allez! Allez!" which I know from my high school French means *go, go* or *go ahead.* I think, *Wow, this is great! I'm going to get in the underground and maybe get back to the States.* I begin to walk over to the wooded area where someone is calling to me. Then I hear bbbbbrrrraaaap-pppp—a machine gun shooting over my head. A group of German soldiers, way down the dirt road I had landed on, were coming after me. If I hadn't landed right in the middle of the road, they wouldn't have seen me so soon. Then I think, *Should I run for it? No way. Those guys would blast me.* So I have to wait till those guys pick me up. And I'm now a prisoner!

I'm put in the back of a van with our tail gunner and turret gunner. Bill, the turret gunner, is lying on the floor of the van because he broke his leg when landing. He had shrapnel in one of his legs and tried to land on the other leg, thereby breaking it. We don't acknowledge each other, because we don't want to let the soldiers know that we were part of the same crew.

Then they separate us, and I'm put in the kitchen in a local farmhouse. Later that day, they transport us to a large structure. It could have been part of an old castle. Anyway, we are put in what I guess was the basement of this building, whatever it was. The place is loaded with other captured American personnel. I'm amazed. There are probably more than fifty other guys there. Nobody gets in a conversation about their experience, because we have been alerted prior to our combat that if we are captured and in a group, there will undoubtedly be German plants within the group to pick up any military secrets that they might overhear. In a way, it's kind of strange, because we know that everyone here (except the German plants) has gone through some unique, personally harrowing experience that would be interesting to hear about.

The next day we are loaded onto trucks with wood benches to sit on and a canvas overhead covering, to be transported to wherever. There are a couple of German guards accompanying us at the back of the truck to keep us from jumping out. I'm kind of at the rear of the truck and keep straining my neck to look through narrow openings of the canvas enclosure to see where we are going. Considering later events, I guess this made the guards suspicious. Apparently, I think, they thought I might be an American spy—having bailed out in enemy territory—to get in the underground to report back to the English or American forces any military targets that may have been camouflaged or overlooked. If not that, then something of that nature. Anyway, we get to our destination and are marched through the streets of some town to what was an interrogation camp. Of course, we are a ragged-looking bunch, and the local citizens look at us curiously, wondering, I suppose, how we (American soldiers) got in this situation.

Anyway we get to the interrogation camp, and a bunch of us are put in a basement cell. There were maybe a dozen or so of us in a cell measuring about six feet by eight feet. Then they take us out individually (in hourly or two hourly intervals) and escort us to our own individual cell, which was really into solitary confinement. I'm the last one to be taken out of the basement cell, and I've been in there overnight. Is it a coincidence that I am the last one to be removed, or is it by design? We are in solitary confinement for another three or four days, with one interrogation session each day. I eventually begin to realize that I was being regarded more seriously due to the fact that later, when all of those of us that were being interrogated were released, within moments of our release, I was again imprisoned, the only one in this group and again assigned to solitary confinement.

In accordance with the Geneva Convention, in those interrogation sessions we only have to give them our "name, rank, and serial number." But the Germans didn't follow the Geneva Convention. They wanted more. At least they wanted more from me. They must have thought I was a planted American spy, and therefore had some military secrets. They must have gotten the idea when they saw me slip my parachute out and over the wooded area (thereby, assuming I had had some previous special training for a special mission) and also when the truck guards noticed me looking out of the truck, in my attempt to ascertain where we were. Eventually, they let all of us out of our cells (that is, out of our solitary confinement).

After my release, I'm sitting there with a bunch of other guys who also had just been released, and then a guard comes up and points to me and says, "Not you," and puts me back into solitary confinement. They apparently wanted more from me than my name, rank, and serial number. What did they want? Some military secret? If so, they were talking to the wrong guy. I didn't have any military secrets. Eventually, I had to tell them where I was from in the States and that I had flown out of England. They finally realized that I was just an ordinary GI Joe and released me from solitary confinement. After that, I felt very guilty, having been forced to give them more than my name, rank, and serial number. This guilt feeling lingered with me for years, even after I was discharged from the service. Prior to that episode, I (as a young kid) had always envisioned myself as a young, tough, macho male. It took me a long time to get over that guilty feeling.

And I never again assumed the tough, macho male attitude. That was gone forever.

Next was our trip from France across Germany, to our luxurious prison camp, Stalag 17B, near Krems, Austria, on the Danube. A bunch of us, maybe a hundred or so, were taken there by deluxe railcar. That deluxe rail-car consisted of a boxcar, with no immediately observable accommodations—just an empty boxcar. The European boxcars are much smaller than ours in the States, maybe half the size. A bunch of us were crowded into one of those boxcars. I can't remember, but I think there were two boxcars. And both of them were loaded with GIs. It was crowed, but still enough room to sit on the floor.

There were no memorable events or noticeable happenings that I can remember on that trip across the various countries. We had a number of pit stops, siding delays, traffic slowdowns, and things of that nature. When we did stop and were let out of the boxcars, there were a number of guards (who came down off the roof of the cars) to watch us during those stops.

You might be wondering what we had for food up to this time in our captivity. I don't remember anything except some dark brown German bread. We each were given a piece, maybe a three-inch cube, once a day. It was hard and chewy, but it must've had a lot of calories or substance in it, because this little piece seemed to nourish us (although we were still hungry) during this initial time of our captivity. I can't remember any liquids at this time, but we must have had some, because I can't remember being thirsty on this trip.

Incidentally, later when I returned to the States, I did some research to find out about how the German prisoners of war here were treated with regard to accommodation, food, and so forth. I was told that they were provided with every thing the normal GI soldier was given—clothes, accommodations in a heated barracks (in the winter time), the same food American soldiers were given (in the same mess hall)—all in accordance with the Geneva Convention. They were treated a lot better than we were treated on this trip and later in the prison camp! It kind of teed me off. But, then again, it wasn't as bad as the concentration camps.

Anyway, continuing our joyride across a big part of Europe in our deluxe railcars (without any notable incidents), we finally arrive at our splendid accommodations in Stalag 17B. The train stopped just outside the gates to the camp. We were escorted into the camp guarded and led to a structure. We are taken into the structure and are told to remove our clothes because we were going to be given a shower. Uh-oh, I'm, of course, aware of the showers they give to the prisoners in the concentration camps. The showerheads in those camps, as we all know now, emitted a lethal gas instead of water, killing all of the occupants for eventual cremation and disposal. I admit I was a little apprehensive at that time. However, I'm relieved when our showerheads dispensed only clear, cool, cleansing water. If I remember correctly, that procedure was part of a delousing process. Thank God.

We get dressed and are led out into the compound, where there are a number of barracks, maybe a dozen or more. These barracks are enclosed with a fence topped with barbed wire and interspaced with guard towers. About fifty feet inside that main fence is the restricted area with a small two-foot high barbed wire fence enclosing a restricted area. If you encroached into that restricted area, you would be shot by one of the guards in the towers. Adjacent to this compound were two other compounds. One of those compounds enclosed Russian prisoners, and the other held English prisoners.

Subsequently, we were led to the barracks that we were to occupy. Inside were a whole bunch of three-tiered bunk beds with straw mattresses, enough to accommodate maybe fifty or a hundred guys. There were already a number of American prisoners there, having been shot down and captured on previous raids. I remember, at that time, that I kind of flopped down and sat on the floor next to one of the bunks, kind of beat, pooped out, and discouraged. I eventually took one of the empty bunk beds to rest and recuperate.

In time, I got to know the lay of the land, so to speak. Our beautiful lodgings consisted of a washroom (no showers), which maybe a dozen guys could use at any one time, and one stove for both cooking and heating. We were provided one bucket of coal per day. The latrine was outside, maybe 150 feet from our barracks. It was just a wood structure over a hole in the ground, with wood seats intended to accommodate the personnel of ten or twelve barracks such as ours. This was all, of course, in accordance with the Geneva Convention—at least in the way the Germans interpreted it.

The images that follow are reprinted with permission from http://www.b24.net. Original photos shot at Stalag 17.

# Historical Information about Stalag 17B

The following information was prepared by Military Intelligence Service War Department 1, November 1945. It was compiled and presented by Greg Hatton, and is reprinted with permission from http://www.b24.net.

AMERICAN PRISONERS OF WAR IN GERMANY
Prepared by MILITARY INTELLIGENCE SERVICE WAR DEPARTMENT
1 November 1945
Compiled and presented by Greg Hatton

STALAG 17b
(Air Corps NCO's)

Location

STALAG17B THE CAMP

Stalag 17B was situated 100 meters northwest of the village of Gniexendorf. This village is located six kilometers northwest of Krems, Austria (48-27N – 15-39 E).

The surrounding area was populated mostly by peasants who raised cattle and did truck farming. The camp itself was in use as a concentration camp from 1938 until 1940, when it began receiving French and Poles as the first PWs.

Strength:

On 13 October 1943, 1350 non-commissioned officers of the Air Force were transferred from Stalag 7A to Stalag 17B, which already contained PWs from France, Italy, Russia, Yugoslavia and various smaller nations. At the time of the first Protecting Power visit on 12 January 1944, the strength had increased to 2667. From then until the last days of the war, a constant stream of NCOs arrived from Dulag Luft and strength reached 4237 in spite of protestations to the detaining Power about the over crowed conditions. The entire camp contained 29,794 prisoners of war of various nations.

*- Reprinted with permission www.b24.net <http://www.b24.net*

AMERICAN PRISONERS OF WAR IN GERMANY
Prepared by MILITARY INTELLIGENCE SERVICE WAR DEPARTMENT
1 November 1945
Compiled and presented by Greg Hatton

STALAG 17b
(Air Corps NCO's)

(continued - Pg. 2)

THE BUNKS

Description:

The Americans occupied five compounds, each of which measured 175 yards by 75 yards and contained four double barracks 100 by 240 feet. The barracks were built to accommodate 240 men, but at least 4000 men were crowded into them after the first three months of occupancy. Each double barrack contained a washroom of six basins in the center of the building. The beds in the barracks were triple decked, and each tier had four compartments with one man to a compartment, making a total of 12 men in each group. Each single barrack had a stove to supply heat and cooking facilities for approximately 200 men. The fuel ration for the week was 54 pounds of coal. Because of the lack of heating and an insufficient number of blankets, the men slept two to a bunk for added warmth. Lighting facilities were very poor, and many light bulbs were missing at all times.

*- Reprinted with permission www.b24.net <http://www.b24.net*

AMERICAN PRISONERS OF WAR IN GERMANY
Prepared by MILITARY INTELLIGENCE SERVICE WAR DEPARTMENT
1 November 1945
Compiled and presented by Greg Hatton

STALAG 17b
(Air Corps NCO's)

(continued - Pg 3)

SHAKING OUT STRAW BUG-INFESTED BEDS

Description:

(continued)

Aside from the nine double barracks used for housing purposes,
one barrack was reserved for the infirmary and the medical personnel's
quarters. Half a barracks was the library, another half for the MOC and
his staff, and half for the theater, a half for food distribution and a half
for Red Cross food distribution and a half for the meeting room. In
addition, one barrack was used as a repair shop for shoes and clothing.
Four additional barracks were added in early 1944, but two other were
torn down because they were considered by the Germans to be too close
to the fence, thus making it possible for PWs to build tunnels for escape
purposes. One of these buildings had been used a s a gymnasium, and
the other chapel. Latrines were open pit type and were situated away
from the barracks.

AMERICAN PRISONERS OF WAR IN GERMANY
Prepared by MILITARY INTELLIGENCE SERVICE WAR DEPARTMENT
1 November 1945
Compiled and presented by Greg Hatton

STALAG 17b
(Air Corps NCO's)

(continued - Pg. 4)

Description:

(continued)

Two separate wire fences charges with electricity surrounded the \area and four watchtowers equipped with machine guns were placed at strategic points. At night streetlights were used in addition to the searchlights from the guard towers to illuminate the area.

GUARD FENCE

Treatment

The treatment at Stalag 17B was never considered good, and was at times even brutal. An example of extreme brutality occurred in early 1944. Two men attempting to escape were discovered in an out of bounds area.

*- Reprinted with permission www.b24.net
<http://www.b24.net*

BETWEEN THE FENCES

AMERICAN PRISONERS OF WAR IN GERMANY
Prepared by MILITARY INTELLIGENCE SERVICE WAR DEPARTMENT
1 November 1945
Compiled and presented by Greg Hatton

STALAG 17b
(Air Corps NCO's)

(continued - Pg. 5)

STALAG 17B - THE OFFICERS

German personnel

Oberst Kuhn - Commandant
Major Wenglorz - Security Officer
Major Eigl (Luftwaffe) - Lager Officer
Oberstabsarzt Dr. Pilger - Doctor

The blame for the bad conditions, which existed at this camp, had been
placed on Oberst Kuhn who was both unreasonable and uncooperative.
Four months elapsed after the opening of the compound before the MOC
was granted an interview with the Commandant to register protests,
and weeks would pass before written requests were acknowledged.
Frequently, orders would be issued to the MOC verbally and would never
be confirmed in writing. Some cooperation was obtained from Major Eigl,
but since there was friction between him and the other German officers
(who were Wehrmacht), his authority was extremely limited.

*- Reprinted with permission www.b24.net <http://www.b24.net*

AMERICAN PRISONERS OF WAR IN GERMANY
Prepared by MILITARY INTELLIGENCE SERVICE WAR DEPARTMENT
1 November 1945
Compiled and presented by Greg Hatton

STALAG 17b
(Air Corps NCO's)

(continued - Pg. 6)

STALAG 17B - THE CAMP

Recreation

The PWs depended a great deal on card games, checkers, chess and other indoor games, as well as reading material from the well-stocked library. A complete public address system with speakers in each barrack inspired the organization of a "radio station" (WPBS) which furnished scheduled programs of music and information

The most outstanding effort in field of recreation was the educational program organized by T/Sgt. Alexander M. Haddon with the following aims and objectives:

(1) To keep men mentally alert
(2) To offer accredited instruction
(3) To help men to plan for post-war educational and vocational activities

Sgt. Haddon was assisted by a staff composed of instructors, librarians, a secretary, and office help. Classes in Mathematics, Laws Photography, Music, Economics, American History, Shorthand, Auto Mechanics, English, Spanish, German and French were given to the students.

*- Reprinted with permission www.b24.net <http://www.b24.net*

AMERICAN PRISONERS OF WAR IN GERMANY
Prepared by MILITARY INTELLIGENCE SERVICE WAR DEPARTMENT
1 November 1945
Compiled and presented by Greg Hatton

STALAG 17b
(Air Corps NCO's)

(continued - Pg. 7)

STALAG 17B - THE CAMP

Relations with authorities

The prisoners regret they are not in an Air Force camp. They consider
that they are entitled to a special camp and the privileges of aviators.
The part of the camp where they are is under the command of an air force
Captain, but he cannot act fully and receives orders from the authorities
of the Stalag. IRCC 1-12-44

While no serious incident has occurred, prisoners are treated badly by
certain guards. They have been threatened and some struck with gun
butts and badly bruised. Spokesman stated that attitude of the guards
is often influenced by bombardments. Commandant stated that no
complaint had yet reached him, but that he would take steps to remove
guards unsuited to their work.

Mail

All mail goes through Stalag Luft 3 and the delay is considerable.
Incoming mail takes 5 months.
Many men captured a year ago have received no mail. Outgoing mail
very erratic. Letterforms issued in order.

*- Reprinted with permission www.b24.net <http://www.b24.net*

# Life in a German Prison Camp

The food supply, at least initially, was meager, usually a piece of dark German bread for each prisoner daily, nourishing but very small. Occasionally, we got some very watery cabbage soup or boiled potatoes. It was just enough to sustain us. However, in time, the hunger pains diminished. We soon became aware of the fact that we didn't need all the food we previously consumed. We all lost weight, the big guys more than the others. I personally lost about twenty-five pounds and stayed stable at that weight. Later the Red Cross got involved. They were able to send us food packages. Each prisoner got one food package weekly, containing (as near as I can remember) a can of Spam, some cheese, coffee, crackers, six packs of cigarettes, and a chocolate D Bar, which was stuffed full of vitamins and other essential nutrients (Historical Documents & Images, p. D33).

Many prisoners used the cigarettes and D Bars for gambling. You could also use those items to trade with the German guards. You would trade for maybe a fresh onion or other fresh vegetables or fruit. The cigarettes were very valuable trade items. Occasionally the food packages never arrived because, I think, the Germans got hungry too, and the shipment of packages kind of disappeared. But even with the food packages we got, we thought and talked about food often, because we began to crave some food items we never got in the packages. I can remember that one time the Red Cross provided some sausage. Not very much, because when it was divided among the barracks, each barrack got a piece about four inches long. It was raffled off in our barracks, and everyone watched the guy who had won to see how he was going to use it. Was he going to just fry it on the stove or put it into a homemade soup? In the end, he just got on top of one of the bunks, where everyone could see him, and just ate it (Historical Documents & Images, p. D34).

One of the prisoners traded, probably with cigarettes, for a crystal (radio set). I don't know if he got the whole set or just the crystal. But with that crystal, he was able to pick up the British Broadcasting Company (BBC), and get unbiased newscasts on the progress of the war. Then periodically, someone would come to our barracks and stand up on a table and update us on the progress of the war. That was great, because we had no idea of how the war was going. When we got news of the Battle of the Bulge in France, I was kind of shook up at that time, because I thought that if we lost the war, I would probably be put to work cleaning up all the bomb mess that would be left after the war was over (Historical Documents & Images, p. D35).

The guy with the crystal could also get some German broadcasts, but those were filled with German propaganda. The guys who came to our barracks would often tell us the difference between the two broadcasts. The difference in progress of our front lines and theirs was usually about twenty miles.

The Red Cross was allowed to provide us with other things, besides food items, such as baseballs, bats, footballs, books for a library, playing cards, and board games like checkers and chess. I got involved in a few chess games, and I consistently beat the other guys, probably because I had played a little bit more in the States than they did. But the Europeans, and particularly the Russians, played a lot more chess in those days (and even now) than we did in America. And on the average, they are much better players than we are.

Because I was beating our guys most of the time, they thought that I was a super-duper chess player. So they set up a game between a Russian player and me. I said, "Hey, wait a minute. I can't beat a Russian player. They are too good!" However, they persisted. I don't know how they got him over to our compound, but here he is. Now I've got to play him. I know I can't beat him in the normal standard style of play, so I think, *If I can introduce something into the game that he may not be familiar with, maybe I'll have a chance to beat him.* There's a standard opening move that ninety-nine percent of the experienced players use: the king's pawn to the king's pawn 2, then the queen's pawn to the queen's pawn 1. But there's another move that's seldom used. It's opening up with the castle's pawn to castle 2. Anyway, it worked. It shook him up a little bit and I beat him. We played a couple of more games after that, but I never beat him again (Historical Documents & Images, pp. D36–41).

Then I got diphtheria, a serious disease that attacks the throat with severe inflammation. I had previously gone to the doctor's office for minor ailments. Usually the wait to see the doctor was one-half to one hour, depending on how many guys were there. This time when I went to see him about my current sore throat, he came out of his office, looked around, and pointing to me said, "You come into my office." No wait. I guess I looked pretty sick. And he was right. I was sick. He swabbed my throat and lit it to see the color of the flame. The test indicated the presence of diphtheria bacteria. He immediately sent me to the hospital, which was on the very top of the mountain. The interment camp was on the same mountain, adjacent to the hospital, but somewhat lower down the hill. They assigned me to a room and, shortly after, came in with a syringe containing at least two quarts of serum and a needle two feet long. Socko—in the butt. This was repeated a number of times during the next few days. That did the trick. I soon felt much better. I had to stay there under observation for the next couple of weeks.

During that observation time, there was a raid on the nearby town of Krems. The raiders are six P-38s. They were the twin-engine double body American fighters that were so effective during the latter part of the war. They were there, of course, to knock out the railroad-marshaling yard in the town. They came in three at a time; the other three staying high above to protect them from enemy fighters. They were capable of carrying bombs as well as guns (fifty-caliber). And I'm sure they also had twenty-millimeter cannons, because it sounded like it. The first three did their thing and then went up to protect the other three fighters as they went down to also blast the yard. On the initial first pass, as they went down into the valley, I'm thinking, *I hope they know that this is an American prison camp and not quarters for a German outfit.* Then I'm thinking to myself, *I'm sure they know that.* The bigwig intelligence guys wouldn't schedule a raid without knowing what's around the target. So I'm standing out in an open area to see what I can see, while everyone else is running for cover.

The first three planes go down into the valley, do their thing, and then make a left turn right over the top of our mountain. It's a sharp vertical turn, just maybe fifty or a hundred feet above the mountain. The pilot can then look down and see me standing out in the open. Then he slowly waves to me while he is in that vertical turn. He knows that he is waving to an America GI prisoner. *They know this is an American prison camp.* Boy, did that make me feel good. They had sent their planes away over here in Austria, and they knew that they would be flying over an America POW camp.

Early in the mornings, a guard would come into our barracks to roust us outside for what we might call roll call. He would come in shouting in German, "Rouse, rouse, gama, gama!" At these times, the guards often had a short conversation with a couple of prisoners who spoke German. These conversations always seemed suspicious to me.

Anyway, we were rousted outside of the barracks to be counted (to be sure no one escaped overnight), usually in three rows with each prisoner lined up directly behind the prisoner in front of him so that they (the guards) only had to count the first row and multiply by three. Very often one or two prisoners may have stayed in the barracks because of sickness, and the guard that roused us out would be aware of how many prisoners were still in the barracks. He could then add that number to the count outside. The guards would then make their report to the commander of the camp. The commander would normally be satisfied. But on rare occasions, he would want the prisoner who had stayed in the barracks during the count to come out so that he could be sure that he was really sick (or injured) enough to have stayed in the barracks. If the commander didn't think the prisoner was sick enough to warrant staying in the barracks during roll call, he would put him in solitary for a few days.

I'm describing this in detail because I was involved in an incident like this. One of the prisoners in my barracks whom I knew well (because he bunked close to me), Bill, had a sore foot one morning and didn't want to walk outside in the mud and get his sore all muddy. But after the count, the commander came into the counting area and wanted to see the guy who hadn't reported outside. Bill's sore didn't look really bad, so he was all shook up because he figured the commander would put him in solitary.

I felt kind of sorry for Bill, because he was really shook up. It just so happened at that time that I had a sore on my foot that hadn't healed, and it was right on top of a nasty-looking birthmark. The birthmark alone is a very ugly skin growth; the combination looked raunchy. So hot-shot me said, "I'll go out for you and show him my ugly sore." In the army, you learn that you never volunteer for anything, but I guess I never learned. I walk out into the compound, and the commander is about a hundred yards from our barracks. As I approached him (and the guard who is with him), he looks mean and angry. When I get to them, the commander asks me why I didn't roll out for the morning count. So I show him the sore on my heel and he reacts. He kind of pulls back, grunts, and makes an ugly face. I might emphasize here that it was a really raunchy and repulsive-looking thing. At that point, he is now of the opinion that this sore was bad enough to confine me to the barracks. So it worked out okay, but I finally learned that in the army you never volunteer for anything. A POW camp is a dangerous place.

Another incident that was memorable was a search in our camp for a prisoner who was a repeat escapee from other camps. He was rumored to be expert at escaping, and he was somewhere in our barracks after his latest break out from another POW camp. He had been captured and was placed in our camp temporarily while the Germans were waiting for the arrival of expert interrogators. (This was the rumor and our assumption; no one really ever told us anything.) The interrogation probably wouldn't have been very pleasant. Anyway, they sent a guard to pick him up, but nobody knew where he was. So they rouse everybody out into the compound while they look for him. We're out in the yard (maybe one or two thousand Kregies, the German word for *prisoner*) while they go through all the barracks, looking into the likely hiding places. They have dogs running around, smelling, barking, and running through and under the barracks. The search goes on for hours and hours while we all stand around the yard. But they find nothing. The weather at the time wasn't too bad; not too cold or too hot. But we were out there for a long time. Finally, they let us back into our barracks. I'm thinking, *How come they didn't find him, with all those dogs running everywhere, up and down the barracks and all over the yard?* I found out later that he had hid in a small space above the latrines where the dogs couldn't pick up his scent. I never knew what happened to him after that. Did someone keep him hidden someplace or did he escape again? I wonder if anyone knows.

After a number of months in the camp (it seemed like a hundred years), and including all these intense experiences in the prison camp, we began to hear slight rumbling sounds coming from the east. In a few more weeks, they became louder and louder. It was soon apparent that it was cannon and mortar shell bursts. We then realized *the Russians were coming!* We knew that it wasn't the American forces because of the radio reports from the BBC station on our crystal radio set. The BBC was reporting that the British and American forces were in the west. I don't think they had even crossed the Rhine yet. At any rate, the Germans, believe it or not, were apprehensive about the situation. They thought that if the Russians overtook our camp that we, the American prisoners, would be in danger. Can you believe that? The Germans were concerned about our safety!

So, as the Russians got closer and closer, they decided to march us out of the camp! We marched westward along the Danube River, away from the invading Russians. Each of us took as much as we could carry, mostly food (primarily what was left of our Red Cross parcels). One great advantage of this movement was the geographical location where we were marching. We marched just adjacent to the Danube River and directly in view of the snowy Alps. It was beautiful scenery. I remember the name of only one city from this journey, a town called Linz.

Our march along the Danube took many days; I figure we marched more than a hundred miles (Historical Documents & Images, p. D42). I don't think we averaged more than ten or twelve miles per day, due to pit stops, lunch, rest, and so forth. So we were on the march for about ten or fourteen days.

None of us had enough food to last for that long, so the Germans would stop along the way and buy or purloin a steer or oxen, slaughter it, and make a barrel of soup or stew to feed the whole group. All in all, there were about 1,500 of us. And, of course, we had no shelter along the way.

Overnight we usually camped out in an open field or a farmer's outback pasture. When it rained, which it did several times, we were miserable. I can remember I was once lucky enough to end up in some farmer's barn we had found along the way. I don't know how I lucked out, but it was great. I slept in a big pile of hay, soft, dry, and warm.

But for the most part, we were hardly ever near a barn or shelter to keep out of the adverse weather elements. So we were always trying to figure out how to build an overnight protection that would keep us out of the rain. Somehow I'd gotten the reputation as a scientific genius and a math wizard, so some of the guys kept asking me to how to design a lean-to so the rain would be diverted away while we were sleeping. However, with the materials available, just tree boughs, there was no way to do that. I thought that maybe if I put the large end of the bough facing the top of the lean-to, the rainwater would have a tendency to run down the slope from the large end. It was an idea, but it didn't work. And we tried the reverse—the large end at the bottom for the lean-to, but that didn't work either. So much for the scientific genius!

What really helped to offer some comfort during this journey were the bonfires we were able to build with dried branches and tree limbs that were scattered around in the wooded areas that we were lucky enough to encounter along the way. The only problem was that we never seemed to find enough dried branches and wood to last through the night, so we often got cold as the fires died while we slept. It got pretty chilly a couple of times.

Another high spot on this journey was a good potato soup that we were able to make from bunches of potatoes that became available to us from time to time. Boy, was that good! All that we had to do was put the potatoes in a pan or empty can and cook them over the bonfires until the mixture became thick and soft. I repeat, boy, was that *good!* It's strange how some minor things stand out in my mind. I suppose it was because I was very cold and very hungry most of the time. When you consider the conditions we all had to endure for those several weeks, it's apparent that we were all close to starving—undernourished and having to live and sleep in the cold and wet weather elements—but when you're in the trenches, so to speak, you don't realize how much harm is being done to your physical body. Plus, it wasn't just me; this was happening to a bunch of guys.

I also remember a frightening experience on this march. A small group of German SS (The SS military branch, the Waffen-SS, evolved into a second German army in addition to the regular German army, the Wehrmacht.) storm troopers came into our campsite as we were preparing to camp for the night. They were armed, mean, scary, and arrogant. In their arrogant manner, they addressed a couple of the GI prisoners. They were speaking German, but the prisoners didn't know what they were saying, so they couldn't respond in the manner the Germans were expecting. That provoked the SS troopers, and I didn't see it myself, but I was told that they started knocking the GIs down. Somehow our German guards were able to persuade the storm troopers to leave the camp. This was a potentially dangerous situation that could have gotten out of hand, so everyone was put on alert at that time.

At one time in our journey westerly along the Danube, we ran across a group of Jewish and/or political prisoners on what appeared to be a death march. We thought we were in bad shape, but these prisoners were really bad off. They indicated to us by hand signals that they were very hungry. In fact, they were starving. We, of course, didn't have much food ourselves, but many of us threw some of what food we did have to them as they passed by.

Our guards, and even their guards (who were armed with rifles) didn't object. Why? I guess they had a little compassion too. We saw that a number of the Jewish prisoners were helping to hold up, carry, and support other prisoners to help them continue to walk. They were all very weak and dissipated, including the ones who were helping the other prisoners. It was obvious that they weren't going to be able to assist for very long. Occasionally, as they were passing, we would hear a rifle shot behind their group. It was the execution of the Jewish prisoners who had fallen behind due to complete exhaustion. As we passed, we saw those prisoners who had been executed, lying along the side of the road. It was gruesome and depressing. Thank God they treated us much better, probably because they knew they were losing the war and would have to answer to our military if they didn't at least attempt to comply with the Geneva Convention rules and regulations.

Anyway, in a number of days, we camped overnight in a heavily wooded area. Somehow I was told (or I assumed) we were in a portion of the Black Forest of Germany; I later found out we were still in Austria. That night it was damp and uncomfortable. The lean-to wasn't much help. It was a long night, and when I got up the next morning, the German guards were gone. Wow! What's going on? We finally realized that the soldiers who were in uniform and walking around throughout the camp were American GIs! We were liberated! We later learned that the soldiers in uniform were part of Patton's 3rd Army! We had heard about Patton and his 3rd Army, but the last we knew he was on the other side of the Rhine River. Wow, did he move fast! Thank God for that! We were liberated early!

So here we are, the first day of liberation after more than a year as a POW in a German prison camp. Of course, I'm hungry, although not starving like the Jewish prisoners we'd seen not too long ago. Now, since we've been liberated, we're not confined to the camp anymore! We're *free!* So some other guys and I figure we'll go and see if we can find some food. As we are wandering around the countryside, we stumble on a rural farmhouse. We're still in our POW clothes, which are beat-up old American uniforms, so the residents at the farmhouse will know we are soldiers. So we knock, we are let in, and we indicate that we are hungry and want some food. They gave us what they had, which wasn't very good, but we are hungry, so we eat a portion of it and leave.

Then we stumble on an American unit of some kind and ask them if they have any food. They give us some of what they have leftover from their C rations. That was good American food. But it wasn't the best of the C rations, and that's why it was leftover from the original C rations packets. Anyway, we're somewhat satisfied, but we then run into another American Army unit. They give us some C ration packets that have never been opened! So, of course, we eat the good part of these C rations. And by this time, we are pretty well full. Then, believe it or not, we stumble upon an army field mess making hot meals. Because of all the C rations, we aren't really hungry now, but this was a hot meal! We haven't had a hot meal in more than a year. We've got to have some. And so we do.

So I'm kind of lying around satisfied now, but then shortly begin to feel very full. That is normal after all I've eaten. I guess my system just wasn't prepared for that much food, and I start to feel very uncomfortable. But for some reason, I don't feel like I'm going to vomit. Now I'm sitting there thinking, *I'm going to die!* I'm not thinking that I may die; I *know* that I'm going to die! Now I'm thinking, *Wow, all the things I've been through in the last couple of years, and now I eat myself to death!* Believe it or not, I was convinced that I was going to die right then and there.

Obviously, I was wrong.

The army then reorganizes us, delouses us, cleans us up, gives us new uniforms, and flies us to camp Lucky Strike in the northern part of France for processing. We are shipped by boat back to the States. Of course, they feed us well, some very good food on the boat trip back to the states. They wanted to fatten us up so that our parents and relatives wouldn't be too shocked when they saw us. We had all lost a lot of weight while we were POWs.

On the trip back, another minor incident sticks in my mind. At some point, the seas got stormy and very rough. I'm never affected by seasickness or airsickness, so the rough waters didn't affect me. Most of the other guys, however, were moaning and groaning and vomiting from seasickness. Anyway, it's chow time and I'm hungry again! The food they're giving us is great, and I'm looking forward to another meal. When I get down to what is normally the chow line, I'm the only one who's there! Apparently, *everyone* is sick but me. Here I am at the front of a long line of counters filled with great food, and I'm the only one there to eat it! After a year of semi-starvation, I'm confronted with a mountain of food! Of course, I eat again, but I don't overeat. I'd learned from my previous experience that too much of even a good thing can turn sickening (Historical Documents & Images, pp. D43–44).

# Kenneth Horrigan and the Veteran's Administration

A few months after I had been discharged from the service, the summer of 1945, I'd learned that U.S. GIs were now being represented in Washington by the "Veterans Administration." *Wow*, I thought, *that's great!* We've now got someone in Washington to speak on our behalf. As I can remember, I immediately went down to the local Veteran's Administration offices to see what it was all about, and to see what the GI Bill was offering that would benefit me. I don't recall the exact conversation I had with the representative I met that day, but I do remember—and I will never forget—his concluding remark to me: "Do you think that just because you were in the service that the government has to support you for the rest of your life?"

Wow! That was enough for me. Although the GI Bill was processed on my behalf, I never showed my face in the VA office again for about sixty years. Ultimately, I did get my college education paid for as a result of the GI Bill, but I never wanted to experience the kind of rejection I'd received at the VA offices again. I had gone to war at the age of nineteen, traveled around the world, fought in a bomber plane, lived in horrible conditions both as a prisoner of war and trudging across Europe on foot for my country, but I was rebuffed when I tried to find out what the GI Bill, which was created for me, might offer.

Then, in 2004, I got a notification from the American Ex-Prisoners-of-War Office, informing me that I was probably eligible for compensation from the government, due to my war service record and particularly because of my time and experience as a POW during World War II.

That year was about the same time that soldiers who had served in the Desert Storm war in the Middle East had been getting press coverage about the after-war emotional trauma, often referred to as post-traumatic stress syndrome. Apparently, some of the World War II veterans had begun to speak up and say, "Hey, we went through that and a lot more!"

The VA sent me a lot of forms to fill out and wanted me to go through a series of physical and medical tests to determine how much compensation I might be entitled to.

I was reluctant. That first rejection had been such a blow, especially after all I'd been through, that I just couldn't bring myself to try again.

The impact of that original rebuff had stayed with me all of my life. I threw the paperwork away.

But the volunteer who was working with the American Ex-Prisoners-of-War Office was persistent. She called again, urging me to collect the benefits that were due to me for the suffering I'd endured for those several years.

Again the paperwork came in the mail, and my wife urged me to pursue the matter. She speculated that it might be worthwhile, and since I was retired, it would give me something to do.

The process was very involved, requiring much documentation, correspondence, many interviews, and medical tests. The process took quite a while, about a year and a half to process the paperwork and to meet with doctors and counselors to obtain their formal evaluations, but eventually, and to my great surprise, I was awarded full compensation.

It was determined that I was a 100 percent disabled American veteran— sixty years later. As a 100% disabled veteran I receive a monthly compensation, comprehensive health insurance coverage and dental insurance coverage.

I don't regret waiting 60 years to communicate with the VA. When they rebuffed me when I was 22 years old, I was so angry that the anger remains with me even to this day. After all I had been through for our country, I just couldn't believe that it meant nothing to the VA.

# Historical Documents & Images

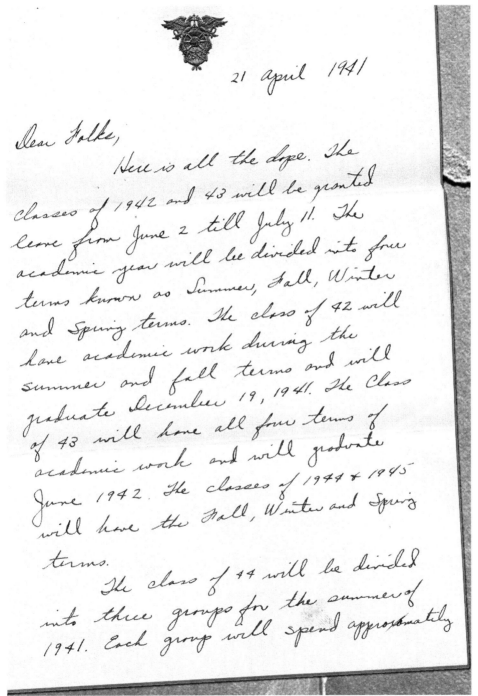

21 April 1941

Dear Folks,

Here is all the dope. The classes of 1942 and 43 will be granted leave from June 2 till July 11. The academic year will be divided into four terms known as Summer, Fall, Winter and Spring terms. The class of 42 will have academic work during the summer and fall terms and will graduate December 19, 1941. The Class of 43 will have all four terms of academic work and will graduate June 1942. The classes of 1944 & 1945 will have the Fall, Winter and Spring terms.

The class of 44 will be divided into three groups for the summer of 1941. Each group will spend approximately

Letter from brother Bob, a student in Annapolis Naval Academy, describing how he will graduate early because of the war. April 21, 1941. Page 1 of the letter.

one third of the summer on leave, One third
cruising out of Annapolis in small craft and
one third honing a modified academic
program at Academy.

It is planned to grant all classes
Christmas leave from about 20 Dec until
3 January.

All midshipmen including the present
incomming fourth class will be
organized as a regiment of four
battalions of five companies each.

I haven't got any dope on June
week as yet, but it will probably
be from May 24 to June 1st.

I received your peanuts and thanks
a lot. We are having nice spring weather
here lately

                            Love
                                  Bob

Letter from brother Bob, Annapolis Naval Academy, April 21, 1941. Page 2 of the letter.

SAN ANTONIO AVIATION CADET CENTER
SAN ANTONIO, TEXAS

August 2 - 43

Dear Mother and Dad—

Well at long last I am in Pre-flight School. It took me a long time to get here but I am not sorry for having spent so much time as a private. I have learned very much, especially since returning from my furlough, that will help me to successfully complete my flying training. Shortly after returning from home I was made permanent right O.D.. It was very educational because I was able to learn about the administration of the army. I can understand, now, a lot of things that seemed foolish and unnecessary before.

Although all the army schools I have been through before were modeled after cadet training none of them were anywhere near being the kind of training we are going to get here. The disciplining system will be tougher and the studies hard and physical training rougher.

Letter from brother Jack, Aviation Cadet Center, . . . 'a rather busy lad' . . . August 2, 1943. Page 1 of the letter.

We will go to school here for nine weeks. We will do no flying. Some of our courses will be; math, physics, code, naval and aircraft identification and several other courses. All this will be combined with guard duty, physical training, drill, mess management (K.P.), and various details. You can easily see that I am going to be a rather busy lad.

Rose Anne sent me a swell Eversharp pen and pencil set for my 21st birthday. I am glad you didn't send me anything because there are very few practical gifts for men in service. The pen and pencil set will come in handy, though. Of course you might send me a chocolate cake if you see one that isn't being used.

Send me all the latest dope about the family. I have been soo busy on my O.D. job I haven't had time to write, "as any plain fool can see".

I am beginning to feel a little like the "cream of the crop" now, rather poor cream, but cream never the less. There was a 35% washout in classification, there will be another 10% washout after Pre-flight, another 35% in Primary and the remaining schools have a relatively small washout rate.

Letter from brother Jack, Aviation Cadet Center, . . . 'a rather busy lad' . . . August 2, 1943. Page 2 of the letter.

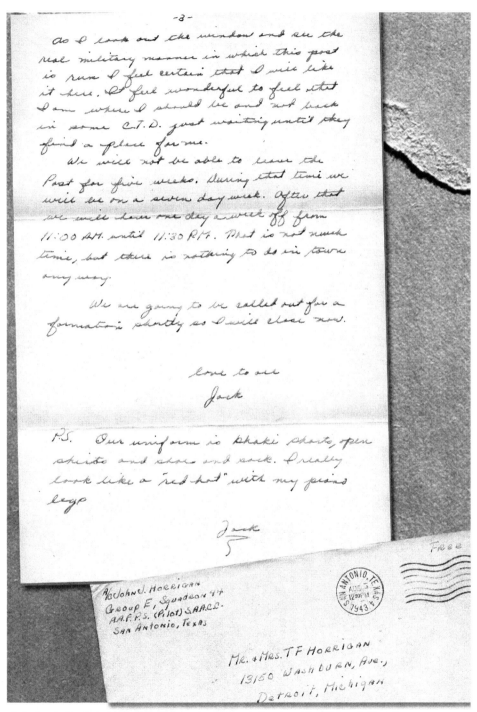

-3-

As I look out the window and see the real military manner in which this post is run I feel certain that I will like it here. It feel wonderful to feel that I am where I should be and not back in some C.T.D. just waiting until they find a place for me.

We will not be able to leave the Post for five weeks. During that time we will be on a seven day week. After that we will have one day a week off from 11:00 A.M. until 11:30 P.M. That is not much time, but there is nothing to do in town anyway.

We are going to be called out for a formation shortly so I will close now.

love to all

Jack

P.S. Our uniform is khaki shorts, open shirts and shoes and sock. I really look like a "red hat" with my pink legs

Jack

A/c John J. Horrigan
Group E, Squadron 44
A.A.F.P.S. (Pilot) S.A.A.C.C.
San Antonio, Texas

Mr. & Mrs. T F Horrigan
13150 Washburn, Ave.,
Detroit, Michigan

Letter from brother Jack, Aviation Cadet Center, . . . 'a rather busy lad' . . . August 2, 1943. Page 3 of the letter.

**FOUR HORRIGAN SONS ARE ALL MILITARY MEN**

And Even Dorothy, Aged 10, Is Anxious for Military Service, Proud Father Declares

Thomas F. Horrigan became a Knight of Columbus March 17, 1918, while he was wearing on his breast the silver wings of a pilot in the World War I, U. S. Army Air Corps, and transferred his membership from Dallas, Texas, Council No. 799, Oct. 21, 1919. The war spirit of the Horrigan family founded then is still rampant, for four Horrigan sons are in the Armed Forces.

"And our daughter, Dorothy, who is 10 years old, is looking forward eagerly to the time when she will be able to join the WAAC's or the WAVE's," Mr. Horrigan says.

The four Horrigan sons are: Lieut. Timothy T., of the U. S. Army Medical Corps, 23 years of age and furthering his education at Wayne University; Ensign Robert P., U. S. Navy, serving aboard the U. S. S. Arkansas; Aviation Cadet John J., taking his flying instruction at Miami, Fla., and Private Kenneth B., in an Army camp at St. Petersburg, Fla.

Mr. and Mrs. Horrigan and Dorothy are keeping the home fires aglow, looking forward eagerly to the leaves which come to the sons, at 13150 Washburn avenue.

And, so far as is known, this constitutes something of a military record among the membership of Detroit Council.

Images, Thomas F. Horrigan, father to Kenneth, Jack, Bob, Tim and Dorothy. A.) Thomas Horrigan, pilot, World War I.
B.) Wedding, Mary Brown and Thomas Horrigan, note: Thomas in Military attire. C.) Thomas and his four sons, 1925.

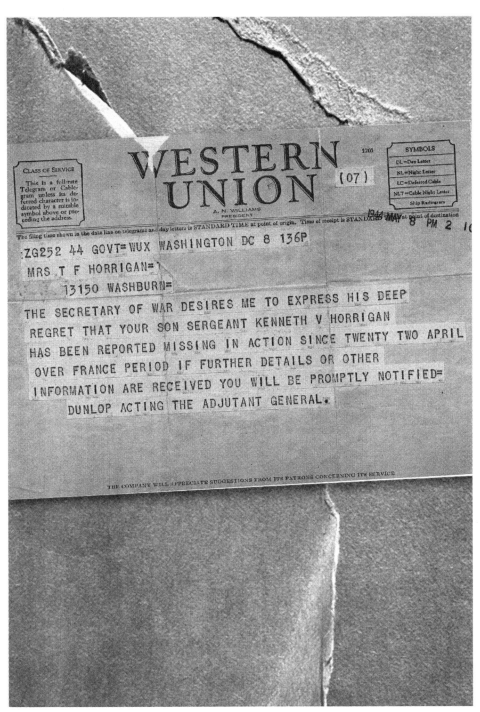

Original Western Union telegram sent to Kenneth's family, April 1943.

HEADQUARTERS
IX BOMBER COMMAND
OFFICE OF THE COMMANDING GENERAL
XXXXXXXX
APO 140

25 April 1944

Mr. Thomas F. Horrigan
13150 Washburn
Detroit, Michigan

Dear Mr. Horrigan:

I deeply regret that your son, Sergeant Kenneth
Vincent Horrigan, is missing in action from the operation
of 22 April 1944. While two parachutes were seen to open
and there is a possibility that your son escaped, I can
offer you no real assurance of this fact.

Please accept my sincere sympathy. Kenneth was a
splendid radio operator and gunner, highly respected by the
members of his crew and all those who knew him. His loss
is deeply felt by his comrades. His devotion to duty and to
our country was unswerving and merited the highest praise.

Again, please accept my deepest sympathy.

Sincerely yours,

*Samuel E. Anderson*

SAMUEL E. ANDERSON,
Brigadier General, USA,
Commanding.

Letter to Kenneth's mother from Samuel E. Anderson, Brigadier General, USA, Commanding, HEADQUARTERS IX BOMBER COMMAND, OFFICE OF THE COMMANDING GENERAL APO 140, April 25, 1944.

*Munitions Bldg. Room 3876*

**WAR DEPARTMENT**

rpv

THE ADJUTANT GENERAL'S OFFICE

WASHINGTON

IN REPLY
REFER TO
AG 201 Horrigan, Kenneth V.
PC-N ETO054

9 May 1944.

Mrs. T. F. Horrigan,
13150 Washburn,
Detroit, Michigan.

Dear Mrs. Horrigan:

This letter is to confirm my recent telegram in which you were regretfully informed that your son, Sergeant Kenneth V. Horrigan, 36,566,935, Air Corps, has been reported missing in action over France since 22 April 1944.

I know that added distress is caused by failure to receive more information or details. Therefore, I wish to assure you that at any time additional information is received it will be transmitted to you without delay, and, if in the meantime no additional information is received, I will again communicate with you at the expiration of three months. Also, it is the policy of the Commanding General of the Army Air Forces upon receipt of the "Missing Air Crew Report" to convey to you any details that might be contained in that report.

The term "missing in action" is used only to indicate that the whereabouts or status of an individual is not immediately known. It is not intended to convey the impression that the case is closed. I wish to emphasize that every effort is exerted continuously to clear up the status of our personnel. Under war conditions this is a difficult task as you must readily realize. Experience has shown that many persons reported missing in action are subsequently reported as prisoners of war, but as this information is furnished by countries with which we are at war, the War Department is helpless to expedite such reports. However, in order to relieve financial worry, Congress has enacted legislation which continues in force the pay, allowances and allotments to dependents of personnel being carried in a missing status.

Permit me to extend to you my heartfelt sympathy during this period of uncertainty.

Sincerely yours,

ROBERT H. DUNLOP
Brigadier General,
Acting The Adjutant General.

Letter to Kenneth's mother from Robert H. Dunlop, Brigadier General, Acting The Adjutant General, WAR DEPARTMENT, Washington, May 9, 1944.

WILL & BAUMER CANDLE CO. LIMITED

MONTREAL, CANADA

May 17th, 1944.

Mr. and Mrs. Thomas F. Horrigan,
13150 Washburn Avenue,
Detroit, Michigan,
U. S. A.


Dear Mr. and Mrs. Horrigan:-

      Just received word about the news regarding your son Kenneth, and take this opportunity to wish you all the necessary courage needed on such occasion, hoping that news will be received very shortly of his safe landing in the presently occupied countries. I will certainly offer a few prayers to his intention and for your good selves.

      I do not want to miss this occasion to state that we are proud of the record of your family, who has so many sons in the different services of your Nation, and only trust that the present conflict will come to an end in a very near future.

      I will always remember the pleasant visit and reception you granted me a few years ago, while I was visiting your City with Mr. Leonard P. Markert.

      With best wishes to you and yours,

I remain,

Sincerely yours,

*Paul E. Tessier*

PET:CL.

Sent to the Horrigan family from Will & Baumer Candle Co. Limited, Montreal, Canada. Kenneth's father was in the candle business, this was a business associate. Will & Baumer Candle Co are in business today, 2009.

Dear Mr. Horrigan —.

Please accept my apology for ... to you sooner. I know how anxious you ... ust recive even my very late news a ... our so ... believe I should start from the very ... eginning.

After the usual preparations we found ours ... airborne and on our way to France on that ... Saturday morning. Everything was goin ... well we finally hit the bombing run and everyone che ... ed in to the pilot. We ran into some Flak and th ... some Flak ran into us. The pilot gave orde ... to abandon the ship. There was nothing to do ... t leave, our right engine was no longer with u ... ... to know your son Kenneth ... anded safely ... ... were waiting for him ... en he came down ... is my pinion that his ... uct on the airplane coupled with that of Sgt ... hman was the only reason Sgt Lomeringe ... able to successfully abandon the a ... raft. I may be wrong but the facts and ci ... mstances seem to point to me that your ... sted cool-ly and the welfare of his comr ... was most important in his mind.

You should be most proud ... son, Mr. Horrigan, he acted as an Ame ... soldier and I want to say he is ... the most

---

Letter to the Horrigan family from 2nd Lt. L. W. Lynch, the co-pilot of the B-26 that Kenneth was on when it was shot down over France. Lt. Lynch escaped into the French underground. This letter is referred to by Dorothy in her introduction as the first confirmation that Ken may be alive. Page 1.

unselfish and brave men I [have had]
occasion to meet. We were ver[y proud of]
him on the crew. Lt. Rinkel, the [pilot], had
only the highest praise for him [on the Atlantic]
crossing. He was due for a promo[tion just be-]
fore our accident, and his con[duct at all]
times was that of a gentleme[n. ... ] Please
    May I ask a favor of [you ...ugh from]
send me his address al[ ... will be]
the looks of things his ma[ ... ]
delivered by a fighting [ ... ]re.
unit in the very near [ ... Lieut Rinkel]
    I have recieved news that [ ...and I'm]
has returned to active servi[ce ...soon]
sure he will write you real[ ... kindest]
    My wife and I send ou[r ... your family]
personal wishes to you an[d ...rom you]
and I do hope I hear [ ... ]
very soon.      Since[re ... ]

Letter to the Horrigan family from 2nd Lt. L. W. Lynch. Page 2 of the letter.

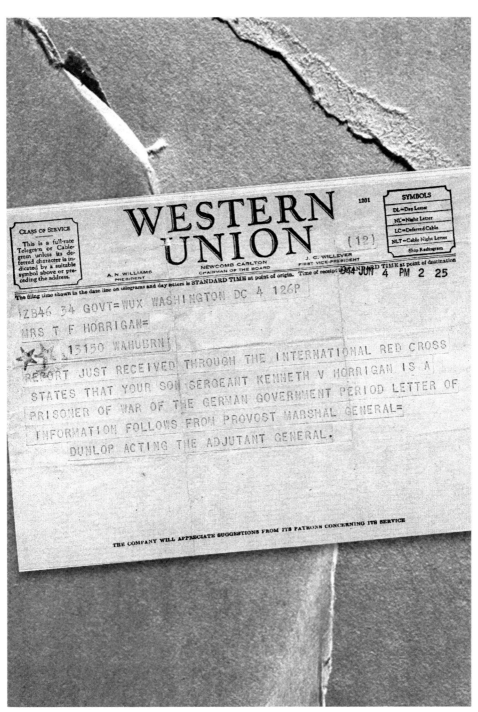

Original Western Union telegram sent to Kenneth's family, June 4, 1944.

## Good News

TOM HORRIGAN, Detroit wax tycoon, has four sons in service.

On April 22, his son K e n n e t h, r a d i o m a n-gunner on a Fortress, w a s reported missing in action o v e r F r a n c e. Last week, by way of k e e p i n g his mind off things, Tom entered the state duplicate bridge tourney. In the midst of the first frame, he was called to the phone, and he came back, beaming happily, but with tears in his eyes. "Win or lose," he announced, "this is the greatest game I've ever played. The War Department has just wired me that Ken is alive . . . and a prisoner in Germany."

Weitzel

\* \* \*

HORRIGAN, Sergt. Kenneth V., Marauder radio operator, captured by the Germans in a raid over France April 22; youngest of four service sons of Mr. and Mrs. Thomas F. Horrigan, 13150 Washburn avenue; previously reported missing.

Horrigan

# Detroiter Is Missing; 3 Brothers in Service

Sgt. Kenneth V. Horrigan, 20, radioman and gunner on a B-26, is missing in action over France, his parents, Mr. and Mrs. Thomas F. Horrigan of 13150 Washburn, were informed today by the war department.

Sgt. Horrigan, a graduate of U. of D. High, is one of four brothers in service. Lt. (jg) Robert P. Horrigan is on active duty in the Pacific; Lt. John J. Horrigan is an instructor at Randolph Field, while Pfc. Thomas F. Horrigan Jr. is a medical student at Wayne University.

## Detroit Flier Missing in Action After Raid

Mr. and Mrs. Thomas F. Horrigan, of 13150 Washburn, received word that their son, Kenneth, 20 years old, has been missing in action following a mission over France on April 22. Kenneth, a sergeant, is a radio gunner. He  Sgt. Horrigan is a graduate of the University of Detroit High School and attended the University of Detroit.

Three brothers are in the service. They are Thomas F., Jr., who is stationed at Wayne Medical College; Lt. (jg) Robert P., on duty in the Pacific, and Lt. John J. Horrigan, an instructor at Randolph Field, Tex.

Newpaper articles saved from local papers. 1944.

ADDRESS REPLY TO
COMMANDING GENERAL, ARMY AIR FORCES
WASHINGTON 25, D. C.

ATTENTION: AFPPA – 8

HEADQUARTERS, ARMY AIR FORCES
WASHINGTON

AAF 201 – (4602)   Horrigan, Kenneth V.
                   36566936

July 24, 1944

Mrs. T. F. Horrigan,
13150 Washburn,
Detroit, Michigan.

Dear Mrs. Horrigan:

For reasons of military security it has heretofore been necessary to withhold the names of the air crew members who were serving
with your son on April 22d.

It is now permissible to release this information and I am
inclosing a list showing the names of those who were in the plane
with your son.

The names and addresses of the next of kin of the men are also
given in the belief that you may desire to correspond with them.

Very sincerely,

*E. A. Bradunas*

E. A. BRADUNAS,
Major, A. G. D.,
Chief, Notification Branch,
Personal Affairs Division,
Assistant Chief Air Staff, Personnel.

1 Incl.

| | |
|---|---|
| 1st Lt. Lloyd Rinkel | Mr. Edward T. Rinkel, (Father) Haviland, Kansas. |
| 2nd Lt. Arthur R. Peterson | Mr. Gust B. Peterson, (Father) Route One, Box 288, Turlock, California. |
| 2nd Lt. Louis W. Lynch | Mrs. Louise A. Lynch, (Wife) 111 Summit Avenue, Jersey City, New Jersey. |
| Sgt. William I. Gomeringer | Mrs. Virginia K. Gomeringer, (Wife) 133 N. Gross Street, Philadelphia, Pennsylvania. |
| Sgt. Kenneth V. Horrigan | Mrs. T. F. Horrigan, (Mother) 13150 Washburn, Detroit, Michigan. |
| S/Sgt. James W. Lehmann | Mr. August W. Lehmann, (Father) 4437 West 58th Street, Maywood, California. |

A letter to Kenneth's mother from the Army Headquarters informing of the other crew members who were serving with Kenneth on April 22 when his plane was shot down. Mrs. Horrigan later received communications from 2nd Lt. Lynch and Sgt. Gomeringer, both of whom escaped.

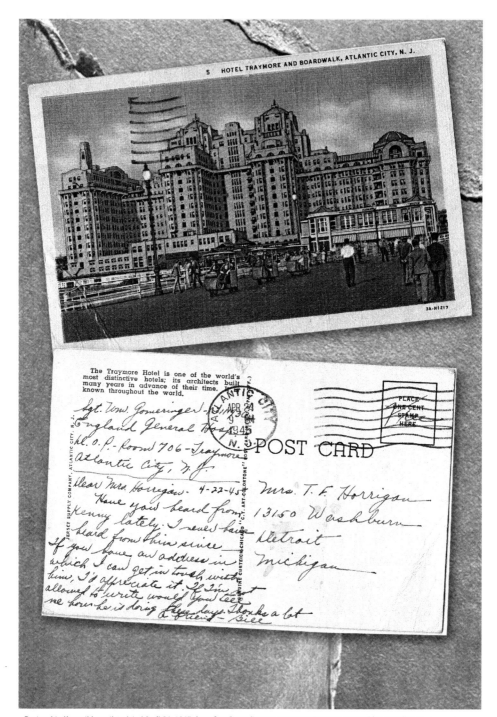

Postcard to Kenneth's mother dated April 24, 1945, from Sgt. Gomeringer, a crew member that escaped into the French underground. Kenneth helped to persuade Gomeringer to jump from the damaged bomber plane when he hesitated in the bomb bay.

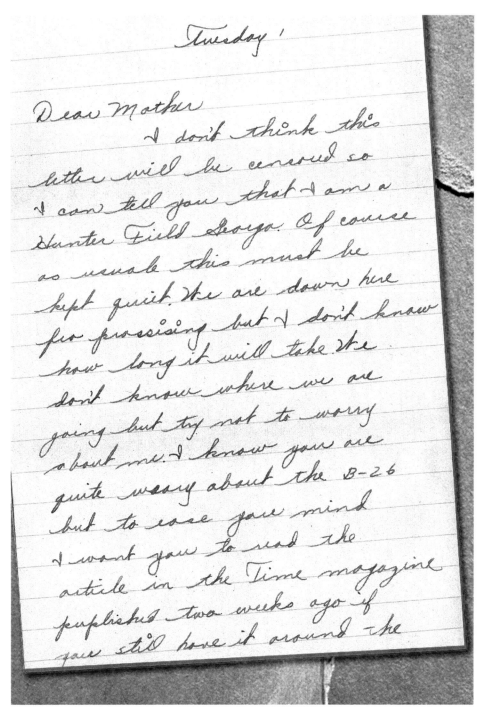

Tuesday

Dear Mother
          I don't think this
letter will be censored so
I can tell you that I am a
Hunter Field Georgia. Of course
as usual this must be
kept quiet. We are down here
for processing but I don't know
how long it will take. We
don't know where we are
going but try not to worry
about me. I know you are
quite weary about the B-26
but to ease your mind
I want you to read the
article in the Time magazine
published two weeks ago if
you still have it around the

Letter from Kenneth to his mother on route overseas, February 3, 1944. Page 1 of the letter.

house.

I went into savanna Georga last night but athought it is bigger that Battle creek I didn't like it as well. I gues it is the typical southern town. They all seem the same to me. Gee— how I wish I were in Battle Creek again — or bring it with me I had more fun in that town than anyother town I have been in sence I was so rudly interupted in my career as an engineer

When I called you up the other night I wanted to tell you that I wouldn't be home again but the lines were taped and I couldn't

Letter from Kenneth to his mother on route overseas, February 3, 1944. Page 2 of the letter.

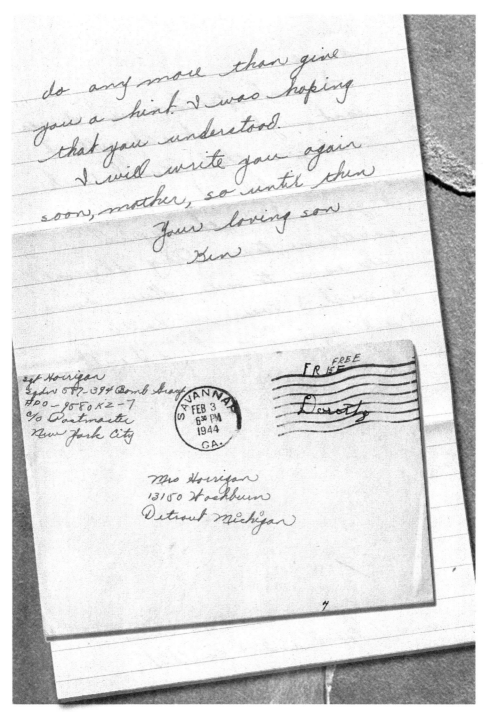

Letter from Kenneth to his mother on route overseas, February 3, 1944. Page 3 of the letter.

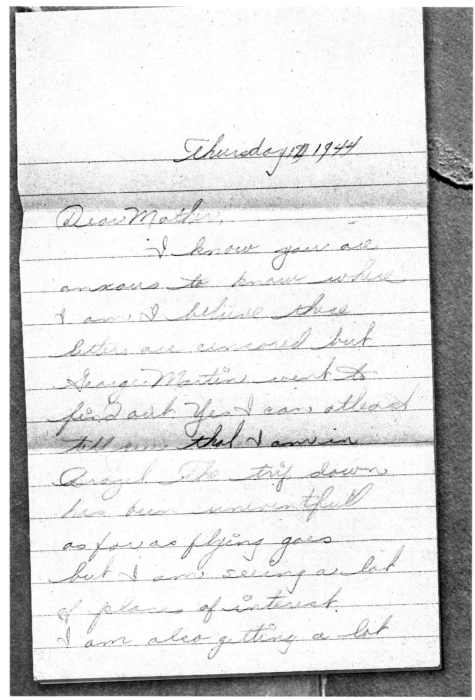

Letter sent on southernly route to Europe, from Brazil, 1944. Page 1 of the letter. Some parts are cut out by Military censors.

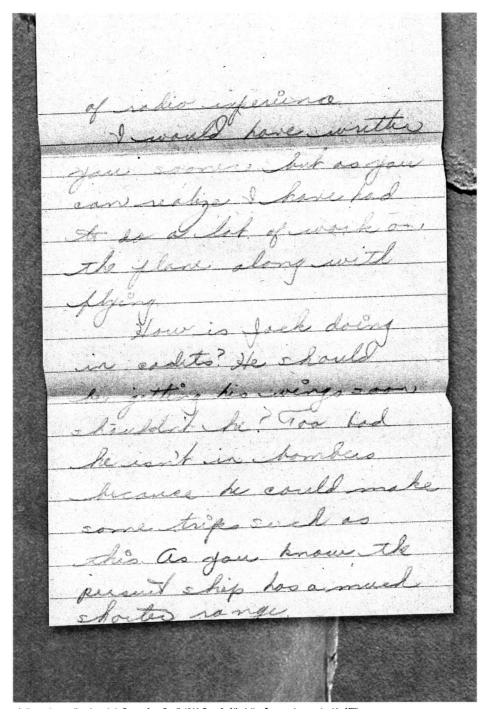

of radio experience
I would have written
you sooner but as you
can realize I have had
to do a bit of work on
the plane along with
flying.
        How is Jack doing
in cadets? He should
be getting his wings soon,
shouldn't he? Too bad
he isn't in bombers
because he could make
some trips such as
this. As you know, the
pursuit ship has a much
shorter range.

Letter sent on southernly route to Europe, from Brazil, 1944. Page 2 of the letter. Some parts are cut out by Military censors.

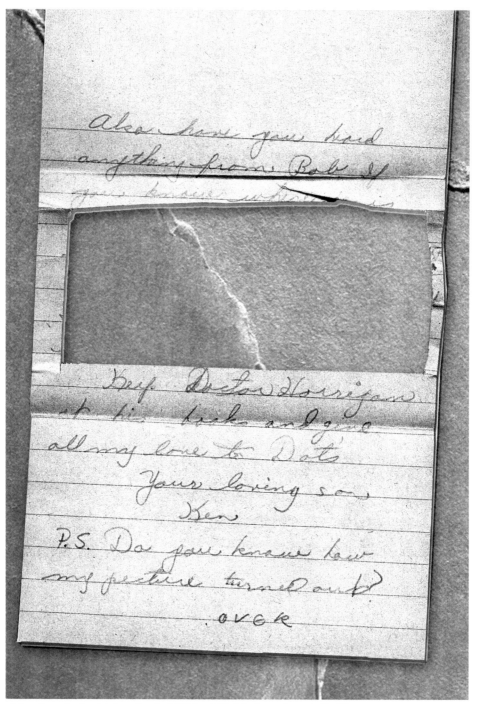

Letter sent on southernly route to Europe, from Brazil, 1944. Page 3 of the letter. Some parts are cut out by Military censors.

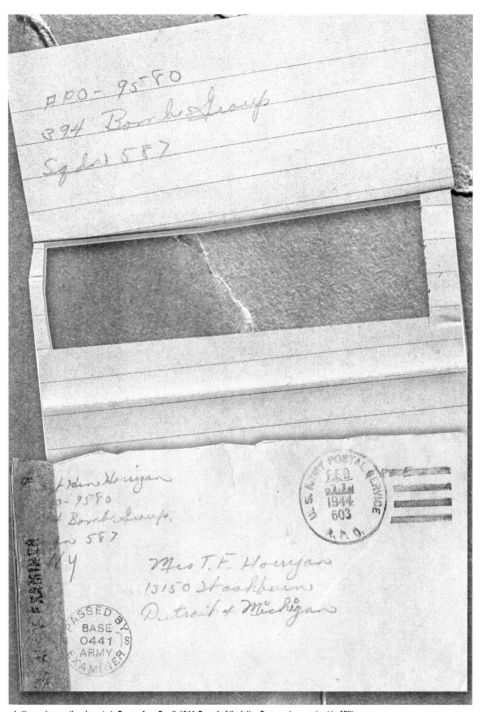

Letter sent on southernly route to Europe, from Brazil, 1944. Page 4 of the letter. Some parts are cut out by Military censors.

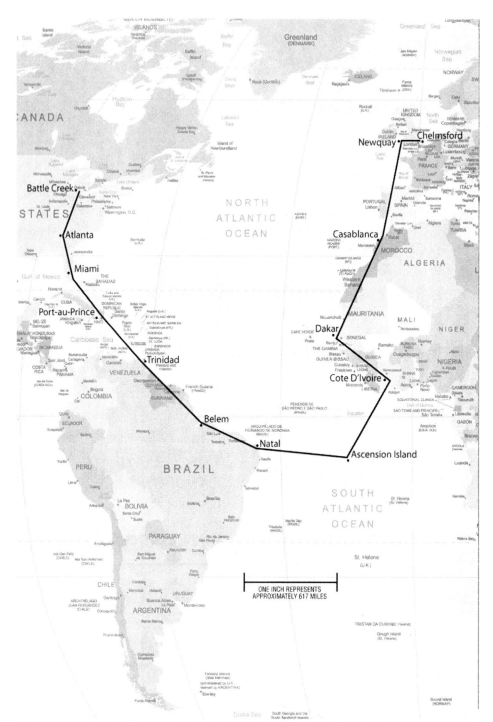

[B-26 MARTIN MARAUDER - MAXIMUM DISTANCE BASED ON FUEL CAPACITY - APPROXIMATELY 1,200 MILES]

March 24, 1944

Dear Mother
          Recieved a letter
from Mary today telling
me that you had recieved
the first letter I had
sent from here. At one
time I planed to send
you a cabel gram but I
thought it might startle
you so I decided against
it although I knew you were
anxious to hear from me.
          I know that dad has
heard by this time heard
that I recieved his letter
which was very welcome
but I didn't write to him
personally because I

Letter sent from location in England. Dated March 24, 1944. Page 1 of the letter.

realize that he must read the letters that I send to you.

I was glad to hear that Bob was put on the California which is one of the new ships. I know when he was first stationed on the Oklahoma that he was rather browned off (army slang) because it was old. Incidently there are a couple of boys in my hut who are from California and you should have heard them when I told them. As you can see I am rather proud of my brouthers and I always tell the boys how they are getting along.

Letter sent from location in England. Dated March 24, 1944. Page 2 of the letter.

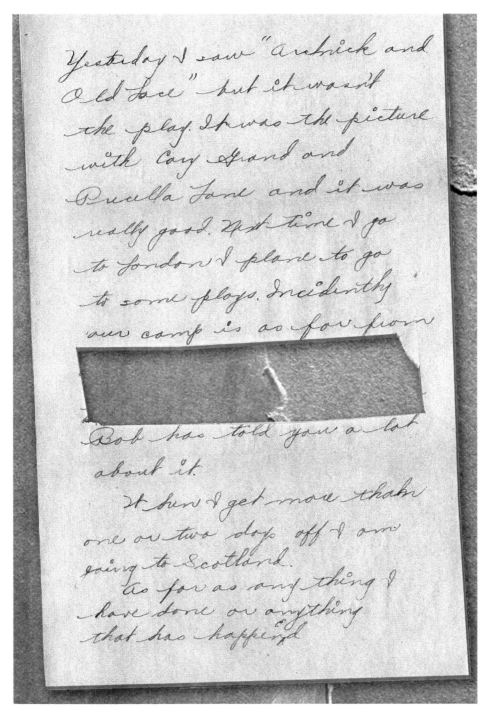

Yesterday I saw "Arsenick and Old Lace" but it wasn't the play. It was the picture with Cary Grand and Pruella Lane and it was really good. Next time I go to London I plan to go to some plays. Incidently our camp is as far from

Bob has told you a lot about it.

When I get more than one or two days off I am going to Scotland.

As far as anything I have done or anything that has happened

Letter sent from location in England. Dated March 24, 1944. Page 3 of the letter.

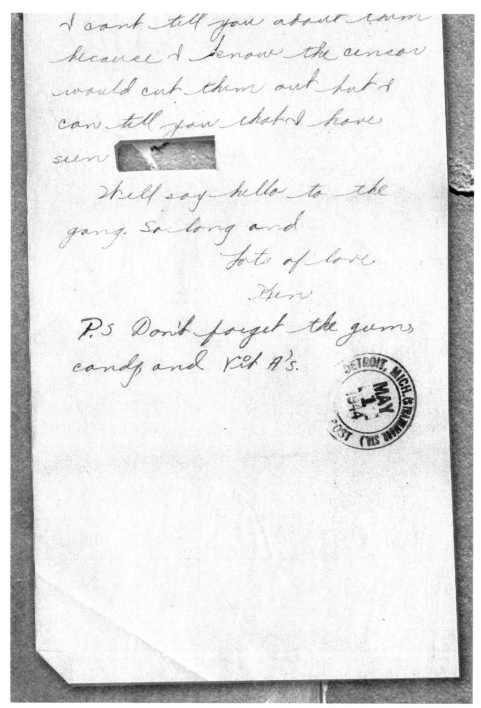

I cant tell you about town because I know the censor would cut them out but I can tell you what I have seen

Well say hello to the gang. So long and

Lots of love

Ken

P.S Don't forget the gums candy and Vit A's.

Letter sent from location in England. Dated March 24, 1944. Page 4 of the letter. Notice the date of the reciept of the letter in Detroit: May 1, 1944 - Kenneth had been reported 'Missing in Action' on April 22, 1944.

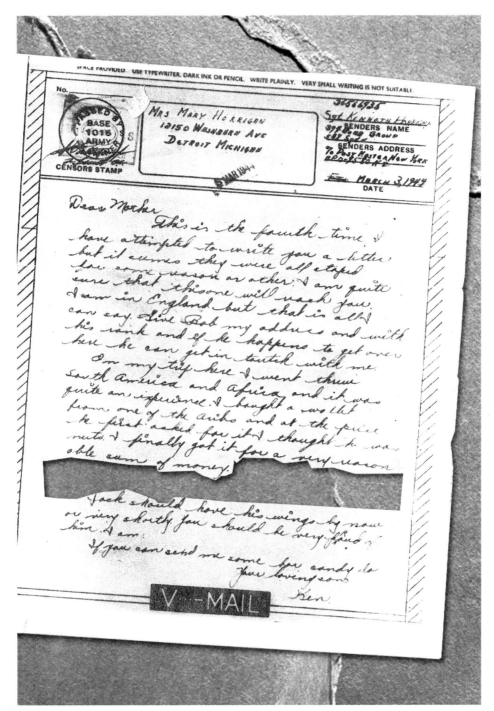

V-Mail letter from Kenneth to his mother from England, March 3, 1944. Some parts are cut out by Military censors.

Tuesday 4, 1944

Dear Mother

Recieved your last letter saying that you had sent me some candy although I haven't recieved it as yet. This is the third time our APO- has chaged. I hope you have noticed that it is now 140.

I was rather surprised to hear that Don Casthe was sent here. No he isn't in my groap because ~~I~~ would have the same APO if he were. In order to find out where he is I will have to go to London.

I just can't ~~seme~~ seem to find anything to write about because almost anything I say will be cut out but I know you want to hear from me so I will struggel along

Letter sent from unknown overseas location. Dated 1944. Page 1 of the letter.

for a couple pages.

Incidently if you send any more pacages of candy or something stick a few magazines such as Riedes Digest in with them. We do get magazines here but not too great a choice. I have read this months Digest.

I don't know Jacks address so he will have to write me first although I do owe him one letter I remember he wrote me once in a — — school and I never answered it.

Incidently are Tom Brennan and Bob Castle still in Italy?

Does Dotes miss me?

Your loving son

Ken

Letter sent from unknown overseas location. Dated 1944. Page 2 of the letter.

B-26 Martin Marauder Bomber Planes in formation over France, 1945.

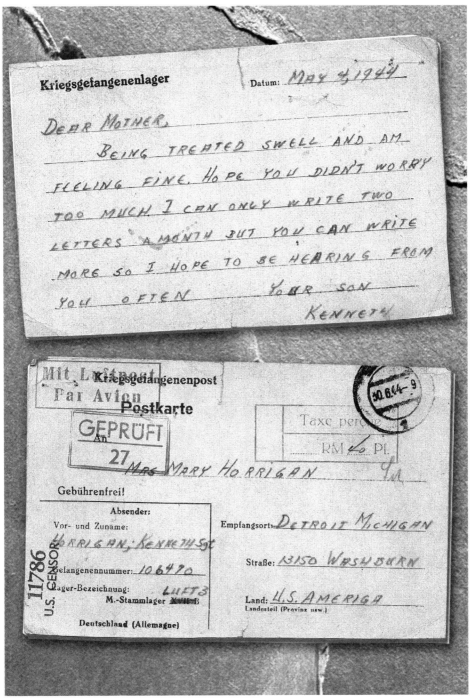

Kriegsgefangenenlager

Datum: May 4, 1944

DEAR MOTHER,

BEING TREATED SWELL AND AM FEELING FINE. HOPE YOU DIDN'T WORRY TOO MUCH. I CAN ONLY WRITE TWO LETTERS A MONTH BUT YOU CAN WRITE MORE SO I HOPE TO BE HEARING FROM YOU OFTEN                    YOUR SON

KENNETH

Mit Luftpost
Par Avion

Kriegsgefangenenpost

Postkarte

GEPRÜFT
27

An: MRS MARY HORRIGAN

Taxe perçue
RM 40 Pf.

Gebührenfrei!

Absender:

Vor- und Zuname: HORRIGAN, KENNETH Sgt

Gelangenennummer: 106490

Lager-Bezeichnung:  LUFT 3

M.-Stammlager XVII-B

Deutschland (Allemagne)

Empfangsort: DETROIT MICHIGAN

Straße: 13150 WASHBURN

Land: U.S. AMERICA
Landesteil (Provinz usw.)

11786  U.S. CENSOR

The first communication sent by Kenneth from the German 'prisoner-of-war' camp, Stalag 17B. The camp was located in Austria, near the town of Krems. Dated May 4, 1944. He had been a prisoner of the Germans now for 10 days and had undergone several frightening interrogations.

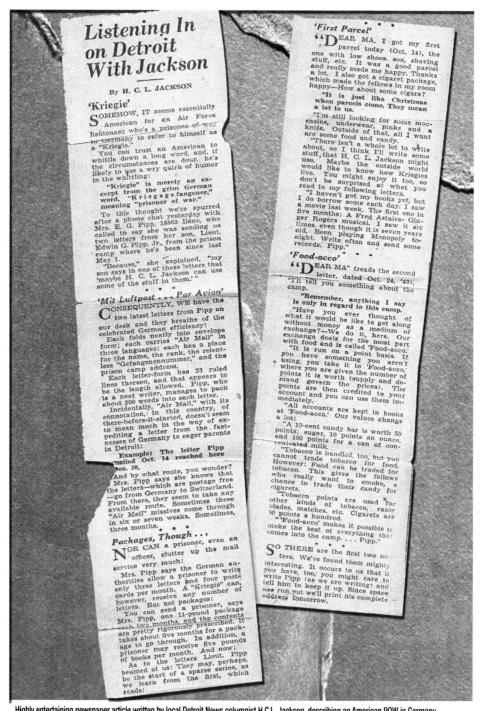

## Listening In on Detroit With Jackson

By H. C. L. JACKSON

**'Kriegie'**

SOMEHOW, IT seems essentially American for an Air Force lieutenant who's a prisoner of war in Germany to refer to himself as a "Kriegie."

You can trust an American to whittle down a long word, and, if the circumstances are dour, he's likely to use a wry quirk of humor in the whittling:

"Kriegie" is merely an excerpt from the grim German word, "Kriegsgefangener," meaning "prisoner of war."

To this thought we're spurred after a phone chat yesterday with Mrs. E. G. Pipp, 18563 Ilene, who called to say she was sending us two letters from her son, Lieut. Edwin G. Pipp, Jr., from the prison camp where he's been since last May 1.

"Because," she explained, "my son says in one of these letters that 'maybe H. C. L. Jackson can use some of the stuff in them.'"

* * *

**'Mit Luftpost . . . Par Avion'**

CONSEQUENTLY, WE have the two latest letters from Pipp on our desk and they breathe of the celebrated German efficiency:

Each folds neatly into envelope form; each carries "Air Mail" in three languages; each has a place for the name, the rank, the relentless "Gefangenennummer," and the prison camp address.

Each letter-form has 23 ruled lines thereon, and that appears to be the length allowed. Pipp, who is a neat writer, manages to pack about 200 words into each letter.

Incidentally, "Air Mail," with its connotation, in this country, of there-before-it-started, doesn't seem to mean much in the way of expediting a letter from the fastnesses of Germany to eager parents in Detroit:

**Example: The letter Pipp mailed Oct. 14 reached here Dec. 30.**

And by what route, you wonder? Mrs. Pipp says she knows that the letters—which are postage free —go from Germany to Switzerland. From there, they seem to take any available route. Sometimes these "Air Mail" missives come through in six or seven weeks. Sometimes, three months.

* * *

**Packages, Though . . .**

NOR CAN a prisoner, even an officer, clutter up the mail service very much:

Mrs. Pipp says the German authorities allow a prisoner to write only three letters and four postcards per month. A "Kriegie" can, however, receive any number of letters. But not packages:

You can send a prisoner, says Mrs. Pipp, one 11-pound package each two months, and the contents are pretty rigorously prescribed. It takes about five months for a package to go through. In addition, a prisoner may receive five pounds of books per month. And now:

As to the letters Lieut. Pipp beamed at us: They may, perhaps, be the start of a sparse series, as we learn from the first, which reads:

**'First Parcel'**

"DEAR MA, I got my first parcel today (Oct. 14), the one with low shoes, sox, shaving stuff, etc. It was a good parcel and really made me happy. Thanks a lot. I also got a cigaret package, which made the fellows in my room happy—How about some cigars?

"It is just like Christmas when parcels come. They mean a lot to us.

"I'm still looking for some moccasins, underwear, pinks and a knife. Outside of that, all I want are some food and candy.

"There isn't a whole lot to write about, so I think I'll write some stuff, that H. C. L. Jackson might use. Maybe the outside world would like to know how Kriegies live. You might enjoy it too, so don't be surprised at what you read in my following letters.

"I haven't got my books yet, but I do borrow some each day. I saw a movie last week. The first one in five months: A Fred Astaire- Ginger Rogers musical. I saw it six times, even though it is seven years old. Been playing Monopoly tonight. Write often and send some records, Pipp."

**'Food-acco'**

"DEAR MA" (reads the second letter, dated Oct. 24, '43), "I'll tell you something about the camp.

"Remember, anything I say is only in regard to this camp.

"Have you ever thought of what it would be like to get along without money as a medium of exchange?—We do it, here. Our exchange deals for the most part with food and is called 'Food-acco.'

"It is run on a point basis. If you have something you aren't using, you take it to 'Food-acco,' where you are given the number of points it is worth (supply and demand govern the prices). The points are then credited to your account and you can use them immediately.

"All accounts are kept in books at 'Food-acco.' Our values change a lot:

"A 10-cent candy bar is worth 55 points; sugar, 10 points an ounce, and 100 points for a can of concentrated milk.

"Tobacco is handled, too, but you cannot trade tobacco for food. However: Food can be traded for tobacco. This gives the fellows who really want to smoke, a chance to trade their candy for cigarets.

"Tobacco points are used for other kinds of tobacco, razor blades, matches, etc. Cigarets are 50 points a hundred.

"'Food-acco' makes it possible to make the best of everything that comes into the camp. . . . Pipp."

* * *

SO THERE are the first two letters. We've found them mighty interesting. It occurs to us that if you have, too, you might care to write Pipp (as we are writing) and tell him to keep it up. Since space has run out we'll print his complete address tomorrow.

Highly entertaining newspaper article written by local Detroit News columnist H.C.L. Jackson, describing an American POW in Germany.

May 12, 1944

DEAR MOTHER

I AM FEELING FINE AND THEY ARE TREATING ME SWELL HERE PLEASE DO NOT WORRY ABOUT ME I AM ON A BASEBALL TEAM HERE. INCIDENTALLY I AM PLAYING FIRST BASE INSTEAD OF SHORTSTOP

I SUPPOSE BY NOW Jack IS MARRIED TO BABE ANN. TELL HIM I CONGRATULATE HIM BOUTH FOR HIS MARRIAGE AND HIS GRADUATION ILL BET HE LOOKS NICE IN HIS UNIFORM TELL HIM HE HAS GOT A BROTHER WHO WOULD ▉▉▉▉▉▉ LIKE TO BE IN HIS PLACE

WELL MOTHER I WILL HAVE TO SAY GOOD BY NOW SO

ALL MY LOVE

KENNETH

The first letter sent from Kenneth from Stalag 17B to his mother, wishing he was in his brother's shoes instead of prison!
Dated May 12, 1944.

**Kriegsgefangenenlager**

Datum: *June 12*

Dear Mother

Today is another nice sunny day and when I finish this I think I will go out and get a little more tan. Give Dorothy my love

Ken

**Mit Luftpost**
**Par Avion**
Taxe perçue
An
RM 40 Pf.

**Kriegsgefangenenpost**
**Postkarte**

18.7.14 10

MRS MARY HORRIGAN

Gebührenfrei
GEPRÜFT 27
Absender:
Vor- und Zuname:
KENNETH HORRIGAN

Empfangsort: DETROIT MICHIGAN

Gefangenennummer: 106470

Straße: 13450 WASHBURN

Lager-Bezeichnung:
M.-Stammlager XI A
LUFT III

Land: U.S. AMERICA
Landesteil (Provinz usw.)

Deutschland (Allemagne)

11786 U.S. CENSOR

A postcard sent from Kenneth from Stalag 17B to his mother, reassuring her that everything was fine. He would have been 20 years old at the time this was written, and had been a prisoner for almost 3 months. Dated June 12, 1944.

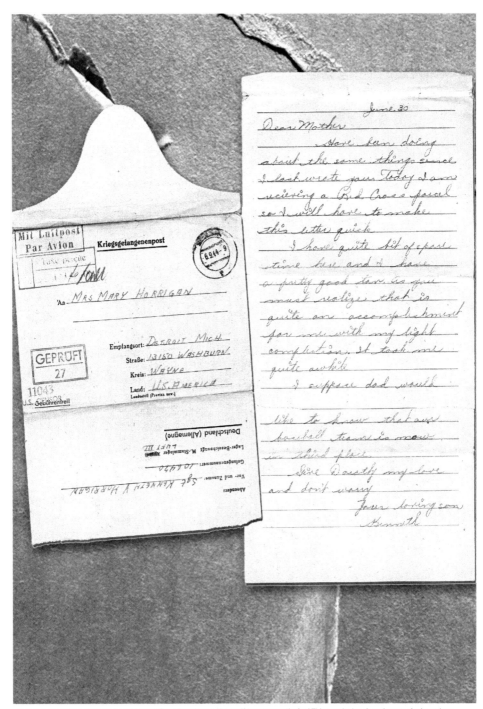

A postcard sent from Kenneth from Stalag 17B to his mother, acting as if he was vacationing! This to calm her down because he knew how worried she was. Acting like everything was just fine, not letting on that he was STARVING! Dated June 30, 1944.

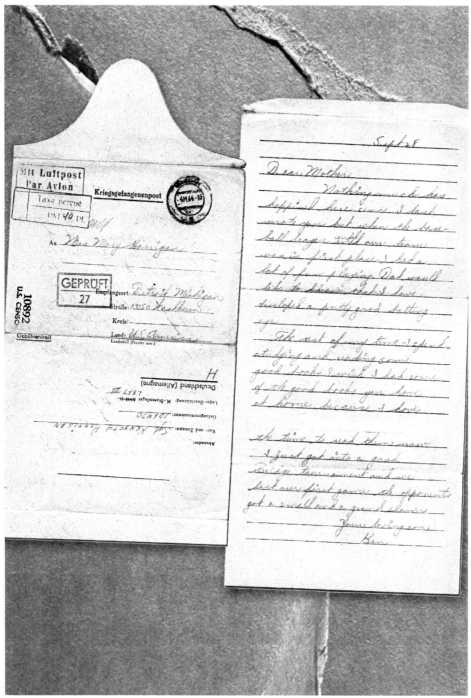

A letter sent from Kenneth to his mother from Stalag 17B, a prisoner now for about six months.
Dated September 28, 1944.

**Kriegsgefangenenlager**                    Datum: *Jan 6, 1945*

*Dear Mother and Dad,*
*Received Dad's third letter*
*and am awaiting parcel. I am*
*comfortable and warm and*
*playing Dad's favorite game*
*"Bridge." Hope to compete with*
*him soon.        Your loving son,*
*Ken*

**Kriegsgefangenenpost**

**Postkarte**

An

**Gebührenfrei!**

Absender:                              Empfangsort: *DETROIT MICHIGAN*
Vor- und Zuname:

*S/SGT KENNET HORRIGAN*

Gefangenennummer: *106470*              Straße: *13150 WASHBURN*

Lager-Bezeichnung: *XVII B*

                                        Land: *U.S. AMERICA*
                                        Landesteil (Provinz usw.

Deutschland (Allemagne)

A postcard sent from Kenneth to his father from Stalag 17B, a prisoner now for about nine months.
Dated January 6, 1945.

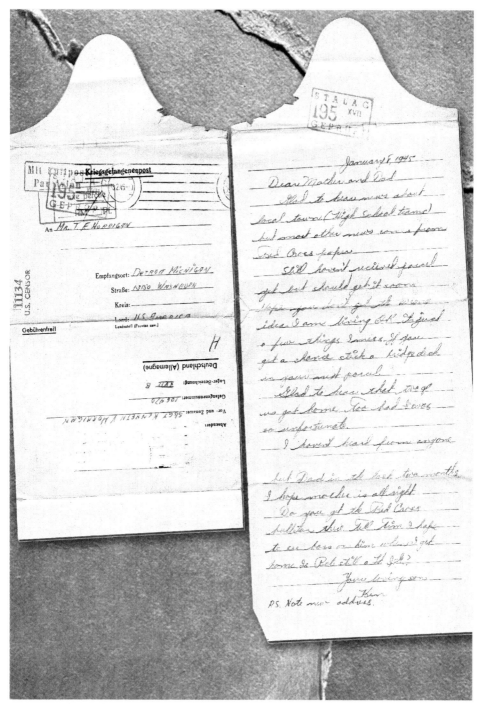

A postcard sent from Kenneth from Stalag 17B to his mother and dad, talking about seeing his brother when he 'gets home'.
Did he know that the war would soon be over? Dated January 8, 1945.

**Kriegsgefangenenlager**          Datum: _FEB 28, 1945_

_DEAR FAMILY,_

_HAVE RECIEVED SIX CARTONS_

_OF CHESTERFIELD CIGARETTES AND ONE_

_PERSONAL FOOD & CLOATHING PARCEL. AM_

_EXPECTING THE OTHER SIX CARTONS OF_

_FIRST DELIVERY SOON AND HAVE_

_RECIEVED WORD FROM YOU OF NEXT PARCEL_

_KEN._

**Kriegsgefangenenpost**

**Postkarte**

An

_MR THOMAS F. HORRIGAN_

**Gebührenfrei!**

| **Absender:** |
| --- |

Vor- und Zuname:

_SGT KENNETH HORRIGAN_

Gefangenennummer _106470_

Lager-Bezeichnung: _XVII B_

Deutschland (Allemagne)

Empfangsort: _DETROIT MICHIGAN_

Straße: _12150 WASHBURN_

Land: _U.S. AMERICA_
Landesteil (Provinz usw.)

A postcard sent from Kenneth to his family from Stalag 17B, a prisoner now for about ten months.
Dated February 28, 1945.

ONE INCH REPRESENTS
APPROXIMATELY 12 MILES

## Evacuation

On 8 April 1945, 4000 of the PWs at Stalag 17B began an 18-day march of 281 miles to Braunau, Austria. The remaining 900 men were too ill to make the march and were left behind in the hospitals. These men were liberated on 9 May 1945 by the Russians.

The marching column was divided into eight groups of 500 with an American leader in charge of each group, guarded by about 20 German Volkssturm guards and two dogs. Red Cross parcels were issued to each man in sufficient amounts to last about seven days. During the 18-day march, the column averaged 20 kilometers each day. At the end of the day, they were forced to bivouac in open fields, regardless of the weather. On three occasions the men were quartered in cow barns. The only food furnished to PWs by the German authorities was barley soup and bread. Trading with the German and Austrian civilians became the main source of sustenance after the Red Cross parcel supplies were exhausted. The destination of the column was a Russian prison camp 4 kilometers north of Braunau. Upon arrival, the PWs cut down pine trees and made small huts, since there was no housing available. Roaming guards patrolled the area and the woods surrounding the area, but no escape attempts were made because it was apparent that the liberation forces were in the immediate vicinity.

The day after their arrival at the new site, Red Cross parcels were issued to every PW. A second issue was made a few days later of one parcel for every fifth man.

## Liberation

On 3 may 1945 the camp was liberated when six men of the 13th Armored Division arrived in three Jeeps and easily captured the remaining guards who numbered 205. Other units of the 13th Armored followed shortly and organized the evacuation of the PWs by C-47 to France on 9 May 1945.

*Reprinted with permission www.b24.net <http://www.b24.net*

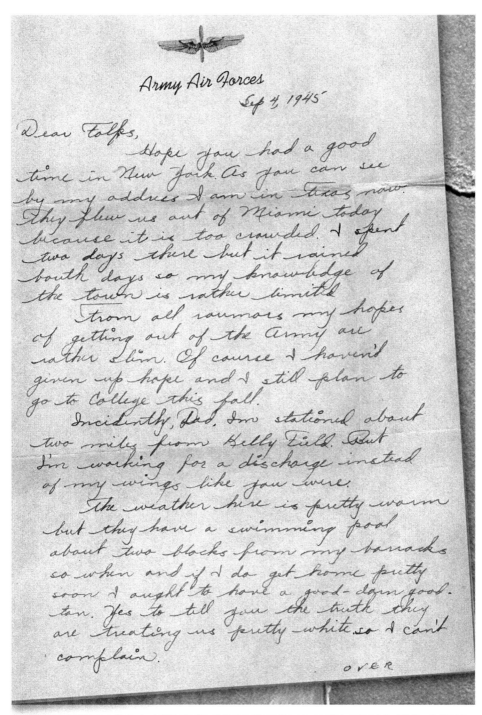

Army Air Forces
Sep 4, 1945

Dear folks,

Hope you had a good time in New York. As you can see by my address I am in Texas now. They flew us out of Miami today because it is too crowded. I spent two days there but it rained both days so my knowledge of the town is rather limited.

From all rumors my hopes of getting out of the Army are rather slim. Of course I haven't given up hope and I still plan to go to College this fall.

Incidently, Dad, I'm stationed about two miles from Kelly Field. But I'm working for a discharge instead of my wings like you were.

The weather here is pretty warm but they have a swimming pool about two blocks from my barracks so when and if I do get home pretty soon I ought to have a good - damn good. tan. Yes to tell you the truth they are treating us pretty white so I can't complain.

over

Letter sent from training camp. September 4, 1945, after Kenneth has been liberated from camp and is back home in the USA. Page 1 of the letter.

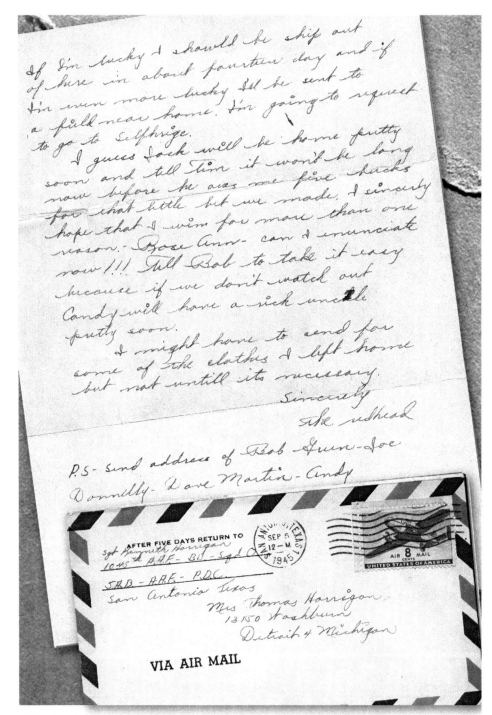

Letter sent from training camp. September 4, 1945, after Kenneth has been liberated from camp and is back home in the USA. Page 2 of the letter.

# A Collection of Letters from a Boy Preparing to go to War

## Brief Military History and Service Record of Staff Sergeant Kenneth V. Horrigan

- Inducted into the U.S. Army on February 3, 1943, (at the age of nineteen) and entered active duty on February 7, 1943, at Fort Custer, Michigan
- Basic training in St. Petersburg, Florida, February, 1943 – March, 1943
- Trained as a radio operator and mechanic in Sioux Falls, South Dakota, March 1943 –June, 1943
- Attended Air Gunnery School in Las Vegas, Nevada, June, 1943 – September, 1943 and was assigned as an Air Crew Member (Radio Operator/Mechanic and Gunner, 587 Bomb Squad, 394 Bomb Group, 9th Air Force)
- Thereafter, participated in Air Combat Training at Kellogg Field, just outside of Kalamazoo, Michigan, September, 1943 – February, 1944
- Flown overseas to England in February, 1944; participated in eleven bombing missions and was shot down by German antiaircraft fire on April 22, 1944, in Northern France, prior to the invasion of Europe by the American Army Ground Forces
- Sent to a German prisoner of war camp (Stalag 17B) April, 1944, in Austria until the war in Europe ended in 1945. Thirteen months later, Patton's 3rd Army liberated us.
- Liberation—On May 3, 1945, the camp was liberated when six men of the 13th Armored Division arrived in three jeeps and easily captured the remaining guards, who numbered 205. Other units of the 13th Armored followed shortly and organized the evacuation of the PW by C-47 to France on May 9, 1945.
- Returned to the United States of America in June of 1945

KENNETH V. HORRIGAN

Letter sent from training camp in St. Petersburg, Florida. February 19, 1943. Page 1 of the letter.

flunk out on my eyes. Although I am
going to apply for it.

I won't get an evening leave until
this Sunday and after that I will get one
every other evening after that. That
is one reason I am writing you.

Will please get me some vitamin A
pills and send them to me. If I don't
pass the physical this first time I can
try later.

I am living in a small hotel with
some forty or fifty rooms in it. And
it is really the berries. Every day I
have been here we have had bright
sunshine and it is just like the middle
of July. I can't wait till I get leave to
roam around this beautiful town.

I wrote Jack a post card the other
day and I imagine he has received it
by now because he is only about 200 miles
from here.

I also received dot's card today
I will write again soon       Ken.

xxx  Kisses for Dorothy

Letter sent from training camp in St. Petersburg, Florida. February 19, 1943. Page 2 of the letter.

Pvt. Ken Horrigan
585 T. S. S
Flight 345

Dear Mother
       I am no longer at
the hotel in St. Petersburg. They
shiped us out to Tent City about
five miles out. It is a lot tougher
than in town but at that it
is not so bad. The city is only
about five weeks old so you can
realize that there are quite a few
inconviencies to cope with. I will
only be out here for about three or
four weeks because it is a camp
where they give you your basic
training (which is mainly physical).
       Aside from that, I was
classified. I am going to some radio
mechanic and radio operators school.
But I was told that if I wanted to
apply for an Air Corps Cadet that
I could do so. I have to get three
letters of recomendation and my birth
certificate. (Please send my birth
certificate to me) after that I will

Letter sent from training camp - 'tent city' outside of St. Petersburg, Florida. February 23, 1943. Page 1 of the letter.

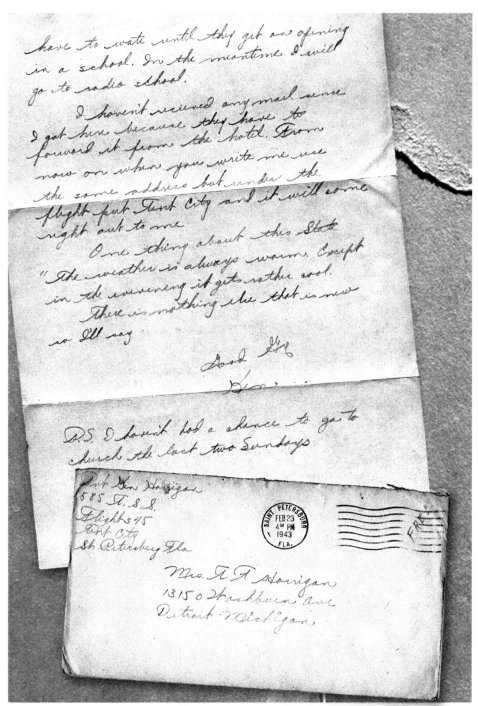

have to wate until they get an opening in a school. In the meantime I will go to radio school.

I haven't recieved any mail since I got here because they have to forward it from the hotel. From now on when you write me use the same address but under the flight put Tent City and it will come right out to me

One thing about this State "The weather is always warm. Except in the evening it gets rather cool. There is nothing else that is new so I'll say

Good Ky

Ken

P.S. I haven't had a chance to go to church the last two Sundays

Pvt Ken Horrigan
585 T. S. S.
Flight 345
Tent City
St. Petersburg Fla

SAINT PETERSBURG
FEB 23
4:30 PM
1943
FLA.

FRE

Mrs. T. F. Horrigan
13150 Washburn Ave
Detroit Michigan

Letter sent from training camp - 'tent city' outside of St. Petersburg, Florida. February 23, 1943. Page 2 of the letter.

March 26, 1944

Dear Dad

Recieved your letter quite awhile ago and it was among some of the first letters I recieved here.

As soon as Jack get his wings I'll be the only man in the family that hasn't got or had a commission. But I guess it isn't the rating that counts anyway.

I guess Jack should be flying in P-40 by now. Sometimes I wish I were in pursuit myself although the B-26 is a swell ship I wish I could tell

Letter sent from training camp. March 26, 1943. Page 1 of the letter.

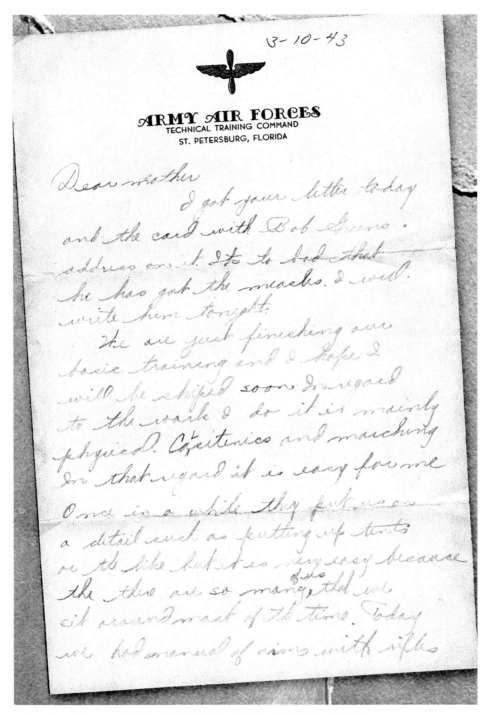

Letter sent from training camp - 'tent city' outside of St. Petersburg, Florida. March 10, 1943. Page 1 of the letter.

Letter sent from training camp - 'tent city' outside of St. Petersburg, Florida. March 10, 1943. Page 2 of the letter.

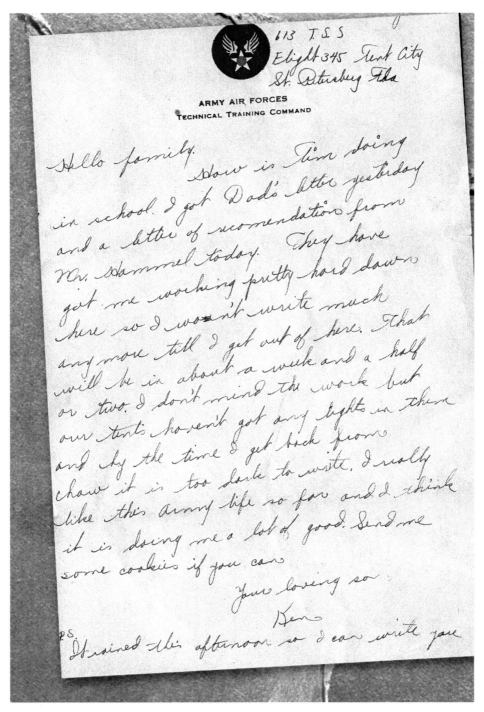

Letter sent from training camp - 'tent city' outside of St. Petersburg, Florida. March 15, 1943.

March 26, 1944

Dear Dad

Recieved your letter quite awhile ago and it was among some of the first letters I recieved here.

As soon as Jock gets his wings I'll be the only man in the family that hasn't got or had a commission. But I guess its isn't the rating that counts anyway.

I guess Jock should be flying in P-40 by now. Sometimes I wish I were in pursuit myself although the B-26 is a swell ship I wish I could tell

Letter sent from training camp. March 26, 1943. Page 1 of the letter.

you about some of the missions I have been on but a course that is impossable. Nevertheless, if you follow the operation of the B-26 in the papers you will have a fair idea of what I am doing here.

I guess you heard that Bob Green finally got in cadets. It took him quite awhile but he finally got there I hope he can make it all the way threw.

If I still like flying after about (restricted) missions I plan to apply for cadet. I hope the war doesen't last that long.

Letter sent from training camp. March 26, 1943. Page 2 of the letter.

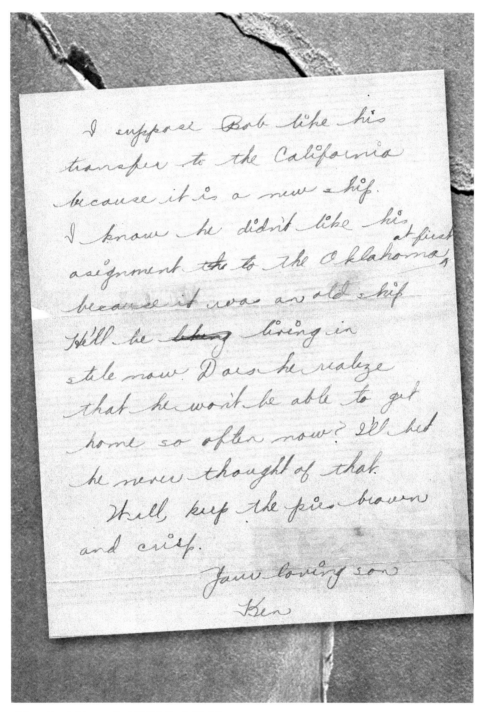

I suppose Bob like his transfer to the California because it is a new ship. I know he didn't like his assignment at first to the Oklahoma because it was an old ship. He'll be living in stile now. Does he realize that he won't be able to get home so often now? I'll bet he never thought of that.

Well, keep the pies brown and crisp.

Your loving son
Ken

Letter sent from training camp. March 26, 1943. Page 3 of the letter.

P.F.C. KEN HORRIGAN
805th T.S.S.
BRKS 1032

DEAR MOTHER,
                    I RECIEVED YOUR PARCELL
IN VERY GOOD CONDITION. EVERY THING
YOU SENT ME WAS IN DIRE NEED. RITE
DOWN TO THE SHOE LACES. I HOPE YOU
DON'T MIND MY PRINTING BECAUSE. I HAVE
TO DO IT FOR CODE AND I NEED SOME
PRACTICE. I DONT KNOW HOW LONG IT
TOOK THEM TO GET DOWN HERE BECAUSE
I DIDN'T LOOK AT THE PACKAGE BUT IT
IS HERE AND THAT IS ALL THAT MATTERS.
THANKS A LOT.

       WELL I HAVE BEEN GOING TO SCHOOL
NOW FOR TEN DAYS AND I NOW CAN
TAKE EIGHT WORD PER MINUIT AND
WAS PUT ON TEN TODAY. THERE ARE
ONLY SIXTEEN OF US ON TEN AND
OBOUT 1/2 THE CLASS IS STILL TRYING
TO PASS FOUR WORDS PER MINUIT
I THINK WHAT I HAD IN SCHOOL
HELPED ALOT.

                         OVER

Letter sent from training camp, Sioux Falls, South Dakota. April 6, 1943. Page 1 of the letter.

I DON'T KNOW MY MARKS IN MY OTHER
SUBJECTS YET BUT I WILL IN A COUPLE
OF DAYS.

IF YOU POSSABLY COULD I WOULD
BE VERY GLAD IF YOU SENT ME ABOUT
THREE SUITS OF UNDER WARE (WITH
THE T SHIRTS). THAT IS THE ONLY THING
I WANT NOW BUT IF THERE IS ANY
THING I WANT I WILL SEND FOR THEM
LATER.

AFTER AWHILE THIS NIGHT SCHOOL
GETS PRETTY GOOD. MOST OF THE
TEACHERS WOULD LIKE TO STAY ON IT
BUT CAN'T.

WELL THAT IS ALL SO GOOD BY

                    YOUR SON

                       KEN

P.F.C. KEN HORRIGAN
805# BRKS-1032

SIOUX FALLS
APR 6
9 AM
1943
S. DAK.

FREE

Mrs. T. Horrigan
13150 Washburn Ave
Detroit Michigan

Letter sent from training camp, Sioux Falls, South Dakota. April 6, 1943. Page 2 of the letter.

April 10, 1943

Dear Mother, I don't always put the date on my letters because I don't always know it. Going to school at night gets you rather mixed up I fact you don't even care what date if is after a while. Now don't get me wrong its not because I don't like the night shift because I do after awhile you get used to it and you also get more time off. I get a 36 hour pass once a week.

I recieved your other package about two days ago Thanks a lot. I can really use them. And the cookies really hit the spot. In your first package you sent me a rosary. Is it blessed?

So Bob and Tim had a nice time. I can understand how. Bob got that nice girl. I could use his uniform Is he still just an Ensign with all his extra duties? About me being made a Corp. I won't be untill I am out of school and maly not them.

About my going to school at night again. I am supposed to sleep

over

Letter sent from training camp. April 10, 1943. Page 1 of the letter.

from 12:30 P.M. until 8:30; eat, etc and
start in school at 10:30. I get out in
the morning at 6:30. I have two classes
of three hours, split up into alternating
classes of 1½ hours each. One class
is code which is receiving the regular
morse code threw earphones. I am
on ten words a minuit (five letters
per word) and my avrage is above
one hundred. there are about 20 of
us on it out of about a hundred or
more students. So you can see I am
doing alright in that co fare. I order
to pass after eighteen weeks you have
to be able to take sixteen words
per minuit. It is getting harder ofcourse.
My other class is the Theory of radio.
In other words theaching you what
condensers, tubes, coils, resistors, etc
do and in general how to fix an build
a radio. Of course I won't be completely
qualified when I get out but if I get
good enough marks I will be able
to goo to another school. I don't know
what my marks are but I think I
am doing pretty good (I hope) I will tell
you as soon as I recieve them.

    I'm glad Tim is working hard
because I realize now — after receiving

Letter sent from training camp. April 10, 1943. Page 2 of the letter.

my marks from U of D that it is best.

Yes I have recieved a couple of letters from Bob Gruen and we are going to try to get together some time if it is at all possable. He knows the day I get off (Wednesday) and if he gets a chance he will fly up.

Is Jack doing any flying yet. And is he still in Georga?

Keep 'em flying

Ben

P.S. I got paid today 30:70 — Other times 10:00 and 18:56 I will try to find out about the bonds. So far I haven't run out of money yet.

Ask all the questions you want I will answer them.

Letter sent from training camp. April 10, 1943. Page 3 of the letter.

4/18/43

Dad,
Well I will try to answer all
your questions and also ask a few
of my own.
My chances of becoming a flying
cadt haven't changed much since
the last time I wrote you about it
except that my eyes are getting better
in spite of my night school. Yes I got
all the letters of recommendation
I get all the money I have needed
so far but if I do need some money
I can cancell a bond and receive the money
in return for it. I get 36 hours a week
to spend it and go to Sioux Falls about
3 miles, with any number a different
friends in my barracks. I go to bed at
12 in the afternoon and get up at 8:00
I start school at 10:30 and go untill
6:30 in the morning. School consists of
one code class and one theory class
devided up into four alturnating periods
with chow in between. School is in
a wooden school house. Incidently all the
boys at this school have had a good high
school educations. Mainly Physics

OVER

Letter sent from training camp. April 18, 1943. Page 1 of the letter.

my marks from N of D that it is
best.

Yes I have recieved a couple of
letters from Bob Green and we are
going to try to get together some time
if it is at all passable. He knows
the day I get off (Wednesday) and
if he gets a chance he will fly up.

Is Jack doing any flying yet. And
is he still in Georgia?

Keep 'em flying
Ben

P.S. I got paid today 30:70 - Other times
10:00 and 18:56 I will try to find
out about the bonds. So far I havent
run out of money yet.

Ask all the questions you want
I will answer them.

Letter sent from training camp. April 18, 1943. Page 2 of the letter.

P.F.C Ken Horrigan
805th TSS-Brks 1082
April 22, 1943

Dear Mother

Instiad of a card I thought
I would write you a litter I was in
town yesterday and today. I had a
tooth ache the other day so I went to
a dentist in town because I know
that the dentist in the army are
putty bad. I thought my tooth was
abseised but when he drilled into
it it hurt a little so it may not
be dead. He took an x ray of it and
I am going back next week

I went swimming at the Y.M.C.A
for about the third or fourth time
and head that I can buy some T
shirts that fit me a little more.

I am now taking fourteen word
per minute (note spelling) and am
the highest in our barracks at 45.

My work in Theory class is alco
all right although I don't know my
marks.

I am waiting for that cakes you
said you were going to send me. I hear
that we are going to get off on
Easter Sunday

Letter sent from training camp. April 22, 1943. Page 1 of the letter.

Have you recieved any bonds yet for me. For that matter have you recieved any for Jack (Incidently how much is he buying?)

I had a couple pictures of myself taken and I will recieve them some time this week. They are only snapshots but if they are any good I think (or I am almost positive) that I can have a photograph made. I could only have two poses made but I will get 6 pictures of each made. I will send two when I recieve them.

I haven't recieved any letters from Rob Green lately. Do you know what is wrong or where he is. I haven't written in a couple weeks because I lost his address. Will you send me his address?

Well that is all that is new so
So long

          Your loving son
                Ken

P.F.C. Ben Horrigan
705-T.S.S.— A.A.F.T.S.
Brks.—1037
Air Base
Sioux Falls
South Dakota

Hi folks'

Well from one
extreme to the other. When I
left Florida the weather
was very warm, and when
I got off here the weather was
very cold.

The food so far has
been very good here — quite a change
from Tink City chow. We are
going to be in quarantine for
about twelve or fourteen days
and then we will start to school.
I hear we are on the graveyard
shift which is means going to school
from ten in the evening till six in the
morning. We don't know how long this
will last. The school will last for
18 weeks and then we will be sent to

Letter sent from training camp. April 27, 1943. Page 1 of the letter.

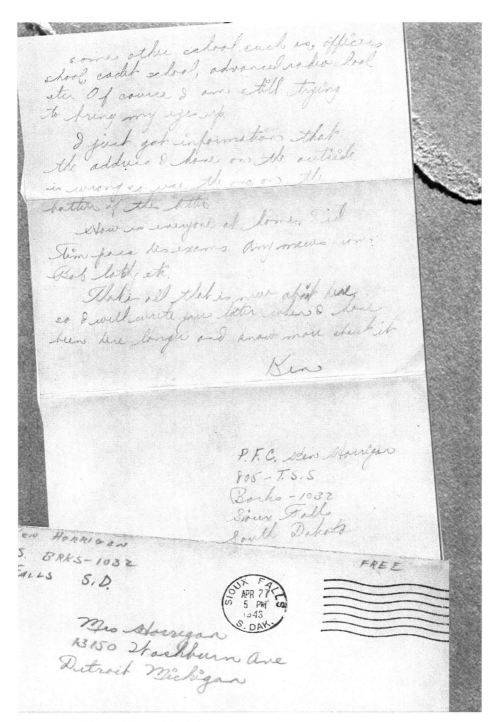

Letter sent from training camp. April 27, 1943. Page 2 of the letter.

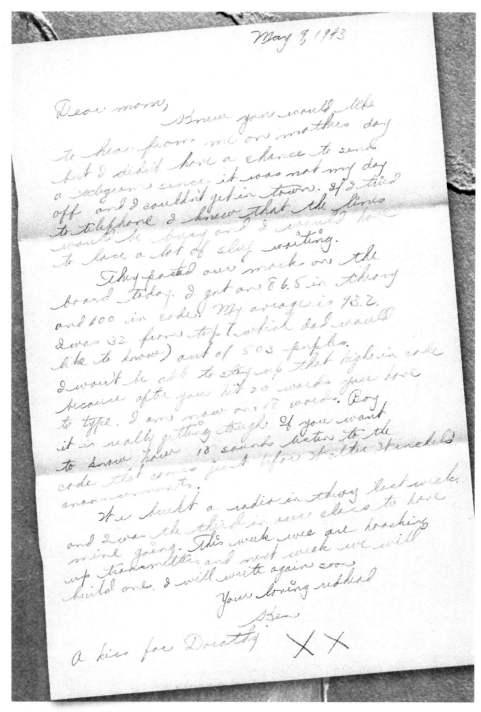

Letter sent from training camp. May 9, 1943

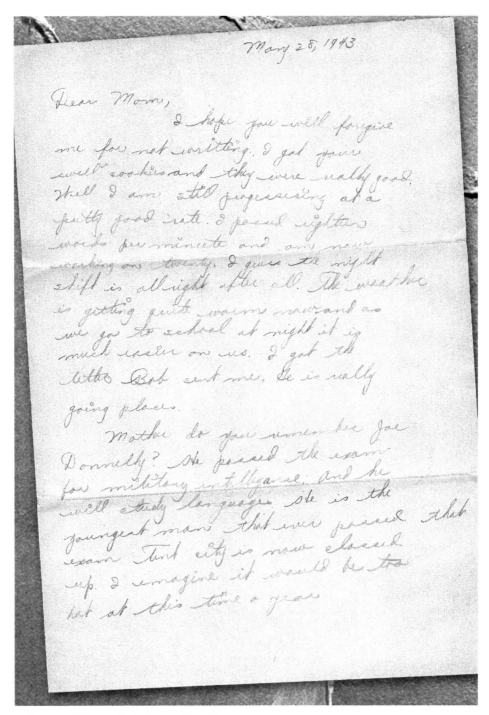

Letter sent from training camp. May 28 1943. Page 1 of the letter.

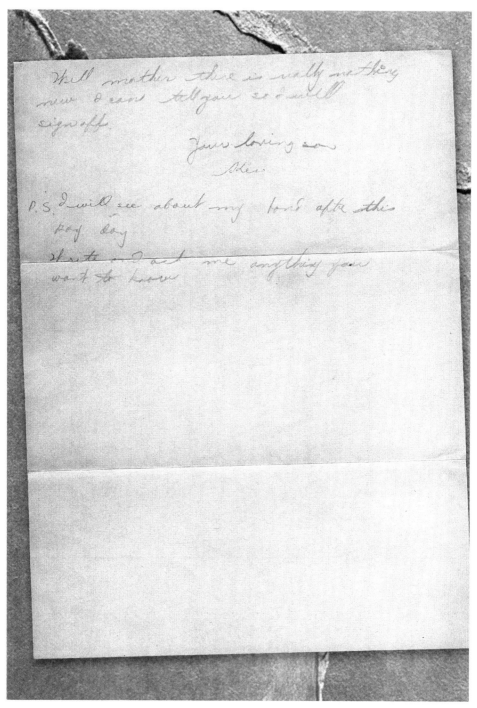

Letter sent from training camp. May 28 1943. Page 2 of the letter.

May 31, 1943

Dear Mother
                Got your letter yesterday.
And got payed today. They aint taking
out anything for bonds so I am
sending home some money for you
to keep for me. Nothing has happened
since my last letter a couple days
ago so I cant tell you anything new.
As for our weather it has been
swell up until yesterday. It rained
all day yesterday but today it is
clearing up.
            I am on the squadron baseball
team (softball) and so far we are
in first place.
            How is Dorothy doing on her
baton lessons and how is Tim doing
in school?
            Well mother I really cant think
of anything to write so I will say
                        your loving son
                        Ken

40 $

Letter sent from training camp. May 31, 1943.

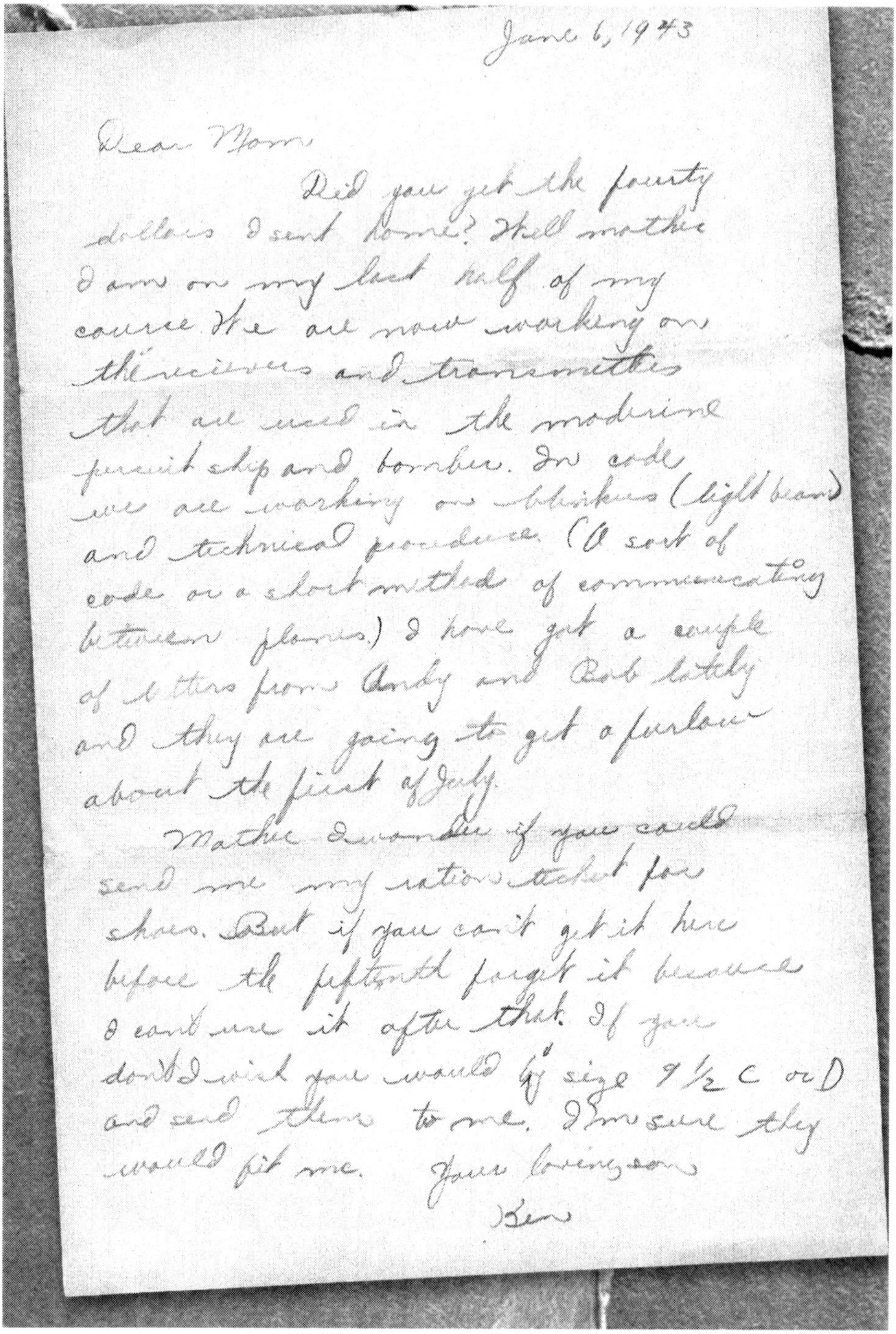

June 6, 1943

Dear Mom

Did you get the fourty dollars I sent home? Well mother I am on my last half of my cource. We are now working on the recievers and transmitters that are used in the modrine persuit ship and bomber. In code we are working on blinkers (light beam) and technical procedure. (A sort of code or a short method of communicating between planes.) I have got a couple of letters from Andy and Bob lately and they are going to get a furlow about the first of July.

Mother I wonder if you could send me my ration ticket for shoes. But if you can't get it here before the fifteenth forget it because I can't use it after that. If you don't I wish you would by size 9 1/2 C or D and send them to me. I'm sure they would fit me.

Your loving son

Ken

Letter sent from training camp. June 6, 1943.

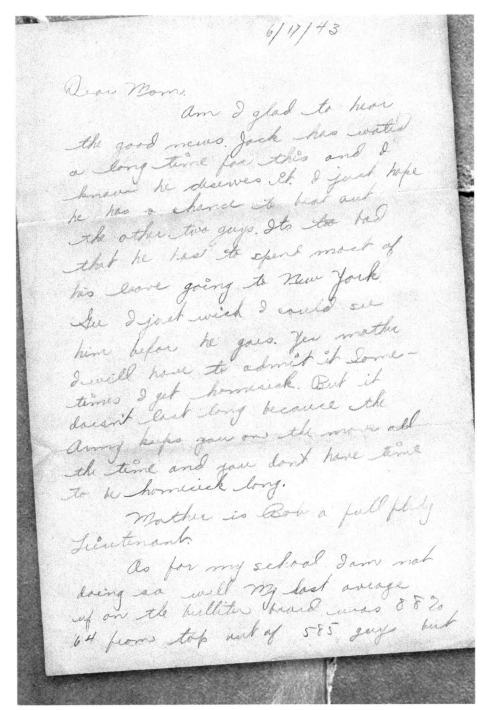

Letter sent from training camp. June 17, 1943. Page 1 of the letter.

it won't be that high next time because I am still on twent wards in code and I got an 80, 85 & 2 in my last three classes

In code the began to mix numbers with letters and when you are used to having numbers in one group and letters in another you get all mixed up. An ex 8 is —... and 6 is —.... and when the come over at 20 word per min. it is hard to tell which is which let alone put it down

Aside from that everything is okay

Thanks for the ration ticket. I want use it for two week (I get paid then) I guess you have enough tickets for coffee until then. If you haven't write send I will send them back and when I need them you can return them.

Your ever loving son,

Ken

P.S. In order to apply for cadet I have to have yours and dad's permission signed by a notary public. I don't need it for about three or four weeks so take your time.

Letter sent from training camp. June 17, 1943. Page 2 of the letter.

7/8/43

Dear Mother,

       This is the first letter I have written you in a long time. The reason I don't write you more often is that I haven't got anything new to tell you. You wanted to know what position I play on the soft ball team. I play short stop. I have played this every day game except the last one. I play played first. We are still in first place and haven't lost a game [...] that was forfeited to the other team because we didn't we didn't know about it.

       Today was my day off and I just got back from town where I was swimming and went to a show.

Letter sent from training camp. July 8, 1943. Page 1 of the letter.

I graduated from this school
in about three weeks. There is
hardly a chance that I will
get a furlow but I will try.
I have a good chance of going
to Radar (Radio Locator). But
of course I cant be sure. I cant
tell you much about Radar
because it is pretty secret.
But is just a method of sending
out a ~~radio~~ radio wave and
locating an enemy plane.
Well mother that is about all
so I will say

Your loving son

Your loving son
Ken

P.S. To bad Jock didn't make
West Point but if Dad works
he might get another chance.
I really was hoping a praying that
he would make it

P.S. My graduation picture. ——→ over

Letter sent from training camp. July 8, 1943. Page 2 of the letter.

Dear Mom

I am still at Sioux Falls waiting for shipment. I might be here for two days and I might be here for two weeks or more. I don't think I will go to Radio. I think I will go to a tower operators school. As soon as I get on the team I will be a Corp. There is a good chance that I will be shiped near Chicago. Of course I am not any wheres sure of these things. You can never tell where you go or what you do next.

Did you recieve my Diploma and graduation book? There was a rumor around here last week that we would ship two by tonite before we shiped but now we are sure that we

Letter sent from training camp. August 3, 1943. Page 1 of the letter.

won't get it
         I got paid this week and
I am sending $20 home. I think
Bob Green has shiped across.
     What is Jack's address now
and how is he doing? Has Tim
got his uniform yet. When he
goes up to Custer it will be
plenty cold. I hope he doesn't draw
K.P. but as an officer of course
he won't
     My new barracks number 1003
                    Your loving son
                         Ken

Letter sent from training camp. August 3, 1943. Page 2 of the letter.

ARMY AIR FORCES
TECHNICAL SCHOOL
SIOUX FALLS. SOUTH DAKOTA

Dear Mom,

I recieved your letter today. Lucky thing. I am shiping out tomorrow morning. Incidently I am very sure I am going to Texas. I also have a good idea what camp it will be and if I am right it is a pretty good. Its possable that I might be able to see Jack.

I am going to be an operator on a plane. I don't know my standing in my class because they didn't give it to us but the first time I was 32 from top and second time I was 36 from top.

Letter sent from training camp. August 13, 1943. Page 1 of the letter.

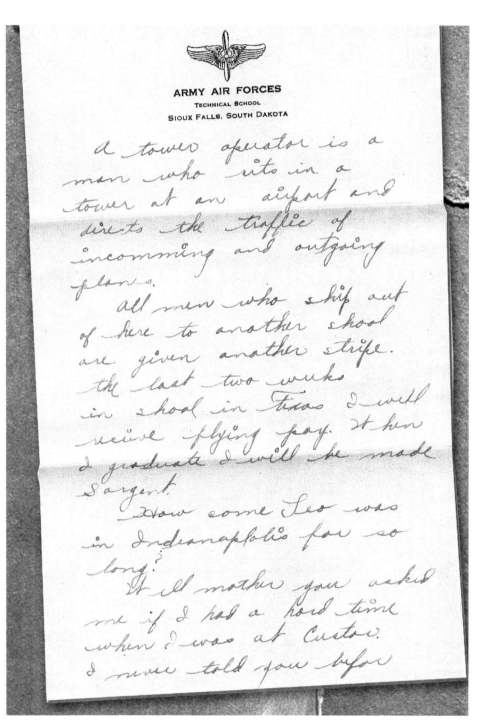

**ARMY AIR FORCES**
TECHNICAL SCHOOL
SIOUX FALLS, SOUTH DAKOTA

A tower operator is a
man who sits in a
tower at an airport and
directs the traffic of
incomming and outgoing
planes.

All men who ship out
of here to another school
are given another stripe.
The last two weeks
in school in Texas I will
recieve flying pay. When
I graduate I will be made
Sargent.

How come Leo was
in Indeanaplolis for so
long?

Will mother you asked
me if I had a hard time
when I was at Custer.
I never told you before

Letter sent from training camp. August 13, 1943. Page 1 of the letter.

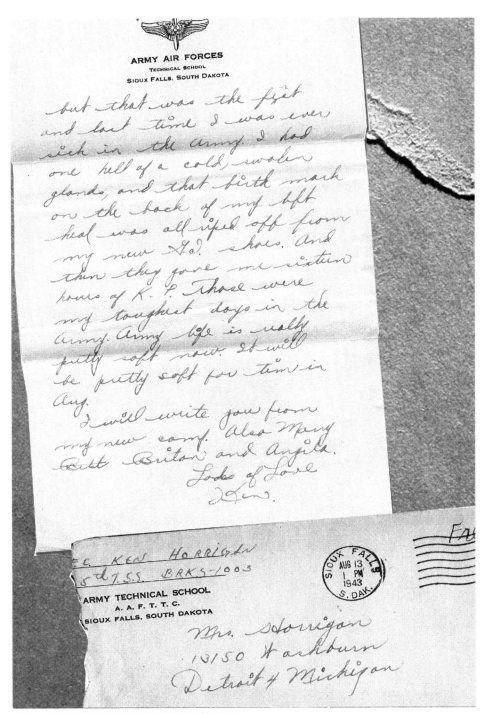

ARMY AIR FORCES
TECHNICAL SCHOOL
SIOUX FALLS, SOUTH DAKOTA

but that was the first and last time I was ever sick in the army. I had one hell of a cold, swolen glands, and that birth mark on the back of my left heal was all riped off from my new G.I. shoes. And then they gave me sixteen hours of K. P. Those were my toughest days in the army. Army life is really pretty soft now. It will be pretty soft for Tim in Aug.

I will write you from my new camp. Also Mary Britt Britan and Angila.
Lots of Love
Ken.

EC. KEN HORRIGAN
5th T.S.S. BRKS-1003
ARMY TECHNICAL SCHOOL
A. A. F. T. T. C.
SIOUX FALLS, SOUTH DAKOTA

SIOUX FALLS AUG 13 1 PM 1943 S. DAK.

Mrs. Horrigan
13150 Washburn
Detroit 4 Michigan

Letter sent from training camp. August 13, 1943. Page 3 of the letter.

Cpl Claude Keebe
37 416085 - 6 y. SS
L.A.A.F.
Laredo, Texas    Tuesday

Dear Mom

     This is considered the best gunnery school in the west. There are quite a few cadets here and for that reason the chow is darn good. They are navigators so Jack hasn't a chance of comming here. They also have a swimming pool here and I have been swimming for the last three days.

     When I told you that I might be shiped near Jack I was going to Harlingen Texas

Letter sent from training camp- Laredo, Texas. Page 1 of the letter.

II

but I was scratched
from that shipment.
I am about two
hundred odd miles from
Los Angeles and the
weather here is just
about the same as it
is there.
I sent some money
to aunt maymie for
your aniversary. I know
it was late but I hope
she used her own
money trusting me to
send some later.
When I read your
last letter saying time
had to do K.P. I laughed
my sides off.

Letter sent from training camp- Laredo, Texas. Page 2 of the letter.

*III.*

I just got back from the decompression chamber. They take you up to an altitude of 38,000 feet. They do this because some men have bad filling in their teeth and the difference of pressure of air inside the tooth and outside cause the air inside to expand exerting pressure on the nerve. Some men also have sinus and that is really bad for high altitude flying. I also took a test for night blindness and I just made it. I have always known that my eyes are

Letter sent from training camp- Laredo, Texas. Page 3 of the letter.

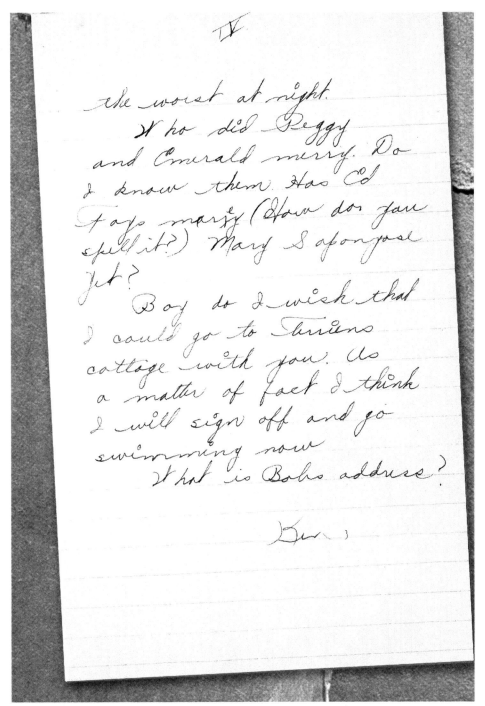

IV

the worst at night.

Who did Peggy and Emerald merry. Do I know them. Has Ed Fays marry (How do you spell it?) Mary S aponyose yet?

Boy do I wish that I could go to Thriens cottage with you. As a matter of fact I think I will sign off and go swimming now

What is Bobs address?

Ken,

Letter sent from training camp- Laredo, Texas. Page 4 of the letter.

Army Air Forces

Sep 4, 1945

Dear folks,

Hope you had a good time in New York. As you can see by my address I am in Texas now. They flew us out of Miami today because it is too crowded. I spent two days there but it rained both days so my knowledge of the town is rather limited.

From all rumors my hopes of getting out of the Army are rather slim. Of course I haven't given up hope and I still plan to go to College this fall.

Incidently, Dad, I'm stationed about two miles from Kelly Field. But I'm working for a discharge instead of my wings like you were.

The weather here is pretty warm but they have a swimming pool about two blocks from my barracks so when and if I do get home pretty soon I ought to have a good-dam good tan. Yes to tell you the truth they are treating us pretty white so I can't complain.

OVER

Letter sent from training camp. September 4, 1945, after Kenneth has been liberated from camp and is back home in the USA. Page 1 of the letter.

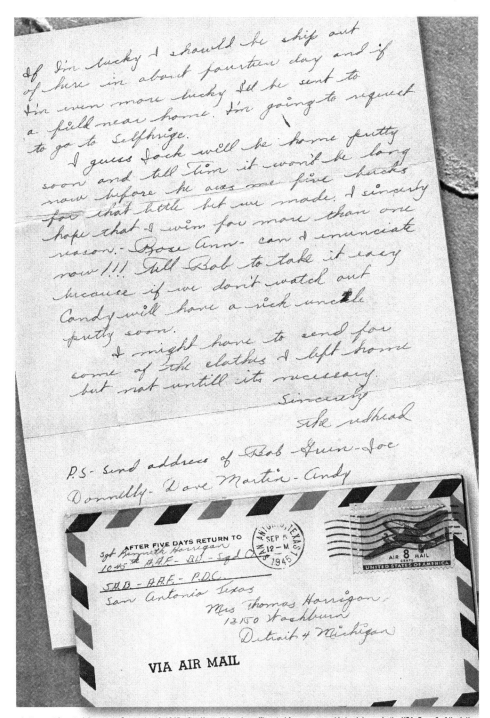

If I'm lucky I should be ship out of here in about fourteen day and if I'm even more lucky I'll be sent to a field near home. I'm going to request to go to Selfridge.

I guess Jack will be home pretty soon and tell Tim it won't be long now before he ows me five bucks for that little bet we made. I sincerly hope that I win for more than one reason. Rose Ann - can I enunciate now !!! Tell Bob to take it easy because if we don't watch out Candy will have a sick uncle pretty soon.

I might have to send for some of the clothes I left home but not untill its necessary.

Sincerely

the redhead

P.S.- Send address of Bob - Gun - Joe Donnelly - Dave Martin - Andy

Letter sent from training camp. September 4, 1945, after Kenneth has been liberated from camp and is back home in the USA. Page 2 of the letter.

Wednesday

Dear Mom,
    I haven't recieved
any letters from home
or I should say I haven't
recieved letters since
I have been at this
field. I have written
six or seven and have
sent 25$ to Aunt
Mayme. I am quite
sure I have put the
right return address
on and the situation
has me a little worried
especially the 25$. It
was for your anniversary
present although it
was very late.

Letter sent from training camp. September 22, 1943. Page 1 of the letter.

I know you will answer this letter and explain

As for myself I have been going to school this last week and you should see how they are craming this stuff in us. In three days I can take a Cal. 50 machine gun appart and put it back together and name ever part and its function – And confidentually I really know it. At the end of the week I will be able to do it blindfolded.

(I am listening to the spotlight band program

Letter sent from training camp. September 22, 1943. Page 2 of the letter.

right now and they all
playing "Lay that pistol
down" right now. How do
you like it?)

One thing I like about
this camp is the fact that
they have a swimming
pool on it. I don't think
I have had a tan in
my life but I have now.
Boy it really look nice.

Well mother thats all
for now so

      Love & kisses

        Ken

I. Incidently how has my
spelling been?

II. I suppose Dots is going
to school

            OVER

Letter sent from training camp. September 22, 1943. Page 3 of the letter.

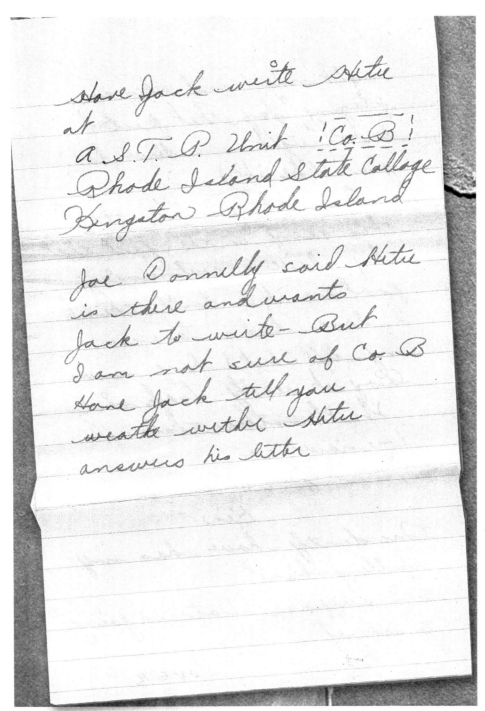

Have Jack write Hitie
at
A.S.T.P. Unit ¡Co. B¡
Rhode Island State College
Kingston Rhode Island

Joe Donnelly said Hitie
is there and wants
Jack to write - But
I am not sure of Co. B
Have Jack tell you
weather withe Hitie
answers his letter

Letter sent from training camp. September 22, 1943. Page 4 of the letter.

Friday

Dear Mother,

You want to know exactly what I do at this school, well I will try to tell you everithing. The first five weeks they teach you all about the cal 50 and cal 30 machine gun. Today I take a test on the 50. I have to take it apart and put it together blindfolded in less than forty minuts. And that won't be easy. They are also teaching us how to operate the Spery ball turret and

Letter sent from training camp - Las Vegas, Nevada. September 25, 1943. Page 1 of the letter.

the general principals of its operation. That is the turret on the bottom of the B-17. You probably think that if I am assigned to a crew that I will be operating it. Well that is wrong. Because I am also studying the operation of the top turret. I am also studying the K-4 sight which works on the same principles as the famous bomb sight. Of course were are just learning the general principles because to learn the whole sight would take years. It is really a wonderfull sight and

Letter sent from training camp - Las Vegas, Nevada. September 25, 1943. Page 2 of the letter.

if you use it right you cant miss. The newest sight is effective up to 1500 yards (very effective) and the best pursuit ship guns are only effective up to six hundred yards. But this sight is only used in the ball turret and upper turret on the B-17.

They are also trying to get us used to shooting all types of guns. I am going at out on the range this afternoon for the third time. The last two weeks we just go up and shoot out of the B-17 and the AT-6. Just to get practice shooting

Letter sent from training camp - Las Vegas, Nevada. September 25, 1943. Page 3 of the letter.

I get a letter from Bob about 2 out of every 3 weeks. I got a letter from him yesterday and he said he passed his mental and physical test for cadets. He will probably get in in about two months.

Seeing as how I passed gunnery test I am quite sure I can pass the test for cadets but I am not going to try until I get out of this school because upon I graduate I will have a sergent rating and seeing as how I am so close I don't want to miss it

Your son
Ken

over

Letter sent from training camp - Las Vegas, Nevada. September 25, 1943. Page 4 of the letter.

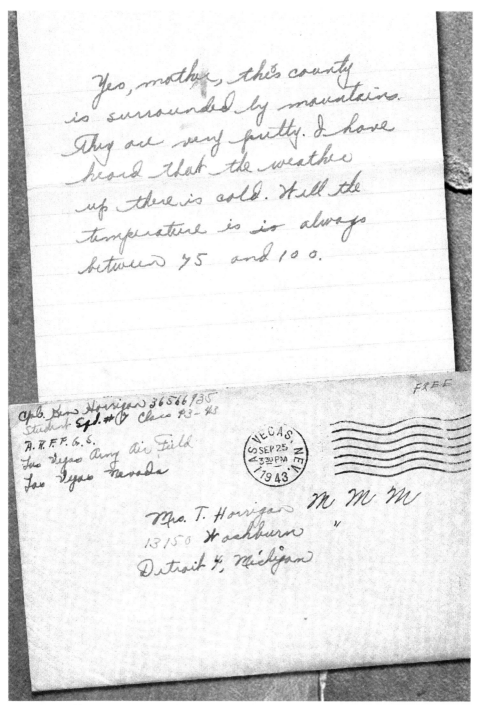

Letter sent from training camp - Las Vegas, Nevada. September 25, 1943. Page 5 of the letter.

~~Fredor~~ Wednesday

Mom,

Recieved your letter with the pictures. I noticed all the freckles on Dorathis nose. I am writting this letter on the flight line wateing to go up. I have been up twice already this week and have shoot four hundred rounds.

You said you were looking for a harmonica for me. I could have told you that you wouldn't be able to get ~~this~~ one. Because all the harmonica's were made in Germany and of course no one has got them on stock anymore.

I am no longer at ~~Indes~~ Las Vegas anymore. I am at Indian Springs. About twenty miles from Las Vegas. But I will be back there next week so keep writting to the same address because it get right to me.

Incidently if you get something for me for my birthday don't send it because I think I will get a fiftten day layover before I ship to my next camp. That will be at the

Letter sent from training camp - Las Vegas, Nevada. October 13, 1943. Page 1 of the letter.

in about 10 days
end of next week. Don't count on
if because, as you must realize,
it is very uncertain. I was expecting
the same thing at Sioux Falls but I
didn't get it. And I am glad I didn't
tell you because I know how
disappointed you would have been.
I will send a tellogram if I get it.

If Jack gets thrue primary he
has a good chance of getting his
wings. About 70% of the men in my
squadron are washed cadets and most
of them washed in primary. The main
reason is air sickness. Has Jack
said anything about it?

If I get home I will tell you about
the cpl. Sgt situation

Your loving son
Ken

Cpl. Ken Horrigan
Student Sqd #7 Class 43-43
P.A.F.F.G.S.
Las Vegas Army Air Field
Las Vegas Nevada

FREE

Mrs. Horrigan
18150 Washburn
Detroit, Michigan

Letter sent from training camp - Las Vegas, Nevada. October 13, 1943. Page 2 of the letter.

Breinigsville, PA USA
13 February 2011
255456BV00004B/1/P